The Coach That's Always There

Inner Wisdom Whenever

You Need It

D1714919

Dr Phil Parker

ISBN: 9798393400378

DEDICATION

For Natasha

CONTENTS

ACKNOWLEDGMENTS

Thanks to all those who supported this book's journey, especially Fiona, Lydia, Manpreet, Bethy and Wren.

INTRODUCTION

THE AMAZON JUNGLE, THE COACH THAT'S ALWAYS THERE AND INNER WISDOM

In 2010 I worked with the extraordinary explorer Ed Stafford. He was undertaking a world record-breaking attempt to be the first person to ever walk the length of the Amazon from its source to the sea. His well-honed skills enabled him to find food and shelter and survive in one of the most remote and inhospitable places in the world, but as he passed the halfway stage a new challenge reared its head. How to deal with the gruelling emotional and psychological demands of a two-year walk full of setbacks, such as running out of funding, the journey taking twice as long as planned and the endless physical exertion, all with the finish line still so far off.

At this point, I was called in as his psychological performance coach. But before you imagine me wielding a machete as I heroically tramped through the Amazon to assist, let me set the scene. Due to the inaccessibility of his location and my complete lack of jungle skills, I couldn't get there to coach him in person and we had to rely on a satellite phone link to work together. We also knew that the satellite signal was unreliable in the region and there would be times when he would need my support but wouldn't be able to reach me. This is where teaching him the tools in this book became invaluable. He learnt how to reconnect with 'The Coach That's Always There' - his Inner Wisdom - *to make skilful choices based on knowing what was right for him*, whenever he needed it. This meant that if the signal went down during a challenging time, he'd be equipped with the skills he needed to find his own way through it.

I've used the book's title 'The Coach That's Always There' as an alternative term for Inner Wisdom here, for reasons that will become clear as you continue reading, although there are many other expressions used to describe this quality. They can range from skill-based practical descriptions, such as, 'That wise voice' to more intuitive,

1

spiritual ones, such as, 'My higher self'. Here's a list of some of the commonest:

- That inner knowing.
- Your internal compass.
- My higher self.
- My inner coach.
- That wise voice.
- My best self.
- The wise me.
- My truth.
- My insight.
- My intuition.

You might have another term that works for you, so to include those too, the book will refer to this quality as 'Inner Wisdom' (IW for short) or 'The Coach That's Always There' and the range of tools to help you access it, as 'Inner Wisdom Techniques' (IWT).

INNER WISDOM - BENEFITS AND PROBLEMS

There are so many benefits to being able to access IW whenever you need it. These include: dealing with situations by focusing on what is occurring rather than being driven by unhelpful past experiences; being able to regroup and start again when we're knocked off balance; making decisions that fit with what we want to achieve in our lives; connecting with how resourceful we are and our immense capacity for change; and so on.

It's an amazing resource to have on our side, however, there is one big issue with IW that many of us have experienced - we're not always as in touch with our IW as we might wish to be. When we look back, I'm sure we can all notice times when we didn't pay attention to that IW; where we made decisions that didn't really fit with what we knew we wanted in our lives; where we made reactive, knee-jerk decisions or where we just couldn't think straight and work out what to do. And often the results weren't that good for us. The purpose of this book is to guide you step-by-step to find your way to tap into the guidance of IW any time you need it.

There are huge benefits to this, as we can see from Ed's experience, as it enables us to find a way through challenging times even when a supportive coach isn't available. And once you've learnt to access 'The Coach That's Always There' through the IWT in this book, you can apply them yourself, tapping into your inner resources anytime you need, whatever comes your way.

Ed finally completed his historic world record and award-winning journey after 26 strenuous and demanding months of extreme exertion, documented in the book and TV series 'Walking the Amazon'. Three elements seemed to be essential to his success. First, his excellent abilities in jungle survival enabled him to cope with the demands of the terrain - without these, he never would have made it out alive. But the second and third elements, the encouragement of his friends, family, and tens of thousands of supporters, and the skills in this book, were also essential to making it through and thriving in the psychologically and emotionally challenging parts of the journey. If they can help in these kinds of situations, then imagine what benefit they could provide in your life.

Sarah, probably like many of you, wasn't a jungle explorer, but she too found the IWT incredibly valuable for dealing with her life challenges. She was a psychologist and used the IWT to recover from a chronic illness and regain her health. Many years later, she wrote to let me know how she'd recently applied the tools to deal with the sudden loss of her father, and how invaluable they had been in that difficult time. In our work together, we'd never discussed using the tools for grief and loss, as our focus had been on health and well-being. Despite that, she recognised how she could adapt these tools to find a way through this new challenge. This potential for applying the same tools to such different situations highlights another of the extraordinary benefits of the IWT. We have all experienced that life can at times be magical and at other times extremely challenging. To have flexible, tailored tools to find your way through both the stormier days and the warm sunny ones, to get the best out of life, whatever it brings to you, is quite a gift. And that is what this book provides for you and your future.

How This Book Works

The book will guide you through a wide range of IWT developed from my research[1,2] over the last 40 years. They'll help you steer your way through every aspect of life more easily. The range is almost endless - from using these skills at a deeply practical level, for example, navigating your way through emotionally charged situations, dealing with people you've found challenging, work-life balance, changing unhelpful habits (eating, drinking, procrastinating, etc.) or getting plans in place, all the way through to a much deeper philosophical, 'What's my life's purpose?' or spiritual level - and everything in between.

All this is set in a framework that explores 4 key areas:

1. Awareness - of what state of mind you're in and how to change it in an instant.
2. Research - on how the brain makes change and the effect these IWT have on our health and well-being.
3. Language - how our words have the power to inspire, keep us stuck and even affect our health.
4. Gateway States - the keys to rapidly unlocking your capacity for change and access to IW. They'll be covered in depth, but to give you some idea of what's ahead on this journey, they are:
   a. Trust.
   b. Inner coach.
   c. Compassion.
   d. Curiosity.
   e. Shift.
   f. Transformation.
   g. Connection.

In each of these areas, you'll be guided through the practical steps of tried-and-tested and simple-to-use techniques. Applying these will make life so much easier and more fascinating as you'll be able to:

- See things more clearly and make better choices.
- Reduce stress and communicate better.
- Let go of outdated habits, limiting perspectives, grudges, and hurts.
- Transform your relationship to criticism and blame.
- Feel more connected and alive.
- Be the best version of yourself even more of the time.
- Shift your inner conversations and trust your judgement.
- Be present to the magic of the simplest things.
- Create exceptional plans, stay focused, and flexibly change them when required.

And in that process, you will develop a deep compassion for yourself and a kindness towards others that, as research confirms[3,4], will make your life happier, healthier and more successful and have a positive effect on anybody that you come into contact with.

Sounds good? Let's get started on developing your IW and connecting with 'The Coach That's Always There', even further.

'Inner Wisdom: Making Skilful Choices Based On Knowing What Is Right For You.'

CHAPTER 1: MY JOURNEY

For many of us, our journey into a new phase of our lives starts with an important life event. As we'll be virtually hanging out for the next few chapters, as a way of introducing what brought me to write this book, I'll begin with my story.

For as long as I could remember, I dreamt of becoming a rock guitarist, and by the age of 20, I was doing well in my musical career, drawing crowds and record company interest, playing the coolest clubs around London, and enjoying everything that went with it. Life was good. One beautiful August afternoon, as the air shimmered in the heat, the bees buzzed amongst the bright, fragrant flowers, and the birds soared against a clear blue sky, in an instant, everything changed.

Moving a caravan, helped by friends, we rocked it backwards and forwards to release it from the rut that held the wheels stuck. Pushing hard on the window to get the heavy vehicle to move, the glass cracked, and broke, and my hands plunged through. My friends at the other end of the caravan were unaware of what had occurred and continued the rocking movements to free the vehicle. This worsened my predicament, and within moments, the shards of the broken window had severed my left wrist. I was rushed to hospital, I'd missed the major arteries, so I survived, but I was left with severe nerve damage. As I was studying to be an osteopath at the time (initially mostly to keep my parents happy) I knew all too well the serious consequences of my injury. The delicate nerves at the wrist must be intact to control the muscles and experience sensation in the hand and fingers. Keen to start my recovery and resume my career, I asked the consultant in charge of my case how long it would be until I could get back to playing the guitar. His answer was clear, 'You will never move your fingers again'. Being a contrary 20-year-old, I demanded a second opinion. The second consultant examined me, 'There is good news', he said, 'Your first consultant was skilled, and his diagnosis was correct. The nerve is damaged beyond repair, you will never move your fingers and you will be left with a useless claw.' So, not quite the answer I hoped for. But I just felt there had to be a way through this. I reasoned to myself, 'If lizards can regrow tails and legs, then surely there must be a way for me to regrow my nerve'. I kept on asking different experts, but all came up with the same 'there's no hope' answers. Disheartened at first, I decided to search for more encouraging stories of how others had overcome similar issues - I found a few that reignited my belief that recovery was possible, including the case of Django Reinhardt, the most famous jazz guitarist of the 1920s, who burnt his left hand so badly he could only move 2 fingers and went on to create a whole new guitar playing style as a result.

Eventually, after many months of seeking even more medical opinions, I discovered a physio working with the mind-body connection who thought I could recover.

And they were right. I did recover, recorded albums, toured and even played with Eric Clapton once, but that's a story for another day...

Even more importantly it led me to research how much these external opinions 'You can/can't recover' and internal conversations 'the experts are right/there must be a way' affect us. This started my research into new approaches in healthcare and my work on IW. It also led to the development in 1999 of the Lightning Process (LP) for helping those with chronic health conditions recover their health. Since then over 25,000 have been helped in 20 countries, 12 peer-reviewed papers, including 2 Randomised Controlled Trials[1,5] and three books have been published on it.

So, even though the story started with a disaster, it was the catalyst that shaped my work and eventually resulted in this book. Looking back on that difficult and challenging time, I think it nicely identifies the central themes of IW, summarised below.

The importance of:

- The power of our inner conversations and beliefs.
- How we respond to setbacks.
- Staying open and curious about new ideas.

- Discovering change may be more possible than we've been told.
- Choosing how we respond to others' opinions.
- Knowing that our nervous system can change and regrow.
- What we learn, and how we can grow, from experiences.
- How our journey might help others.

Throughout the book, you'll be developing your understanding and access to these skills, discovering others' journeys, trying out some fascinating exercises, and thought experiments and mastering a range of IWT that allow you to connect with 'The Coach That's Always There'. Let's begin by exploring how the nervous system and brain makes change.

'Knowing Yourself Is The Beginning Of All Wisdom.' - Aristotle

CHAPTER 2: YOUR BRAIN LOVES CHANGE

Some of you reading this will already have quite a good understanding of the way the brain and nervous system work, but for others, it may be a bit more of a distant or incomplete memory from your days in education. I will be introducing some fascinating research about how change occurs in the body and brain, so to begin with, let's get the basic map of 'the brain and what it does' straightened out first. You'll find the word 'neurology' throughout the book. It refers to our brain and the internal 'wiring' we have that connects it to every part of our body. This superfast communication network of nerves (the cells that make up these 'wires') allows the brain to monitor and respond to what's going on in the body. This system is responsible for a huge range of things within our bodies, these include:

1. Managing our physical movements. That includes both the conscious movements that we choose to do, such as deciding to pick up a cup, and the unconscious ones that we're not aware of much of the time, such as blinking, breathing, and the movement of the muscles that squeeze our food through our digestive system.
2. Sensing things, such as what we see, hear, taste, the air temperature, our hunger, blood pressure, blood sugar levels, etc.
3. Processing information from inside and outside our body and working out how to respond to it.
4. Producing hormones. These are the chemical messengers like oestrogen, adrenaline etc. that give the cells of the body specific instructions, like: 'release an egg now', 'speed up our heart rate by 20%'.
5. Managing body rhythms, such as sleep, breathing, etc.
6. Thinking, communicating, planning, making evaluations and judgements, and, of course, generating emotions.

Yes, it's kept pretty busy with this to-do list.

CAN THE BRAIN CHANGE?

In the past, we used to think that the nervous system was much like an electrical circuit you'd find inside a TV. The wires were burnt into the circuit board in a factory, connecting the components in a specific and unchangeable way to form the electrical system of the TV.

Recent research shows that although the nerve cells do act a lot like wires, transmitting electrical signals like the TV's wires, this circuit board model isn't a good enough representation of how the brain actually works. This is because the wires of the nervous system, the nerves, are living tissue. They are not fixed or unchangeable like the wires in the TV, instead, they can change their shape, length, and position and so unlike the TV's wires, they can make new connections with other nerves, creating new circuits. This means a signal that has always been sent to a particular nerve, producing a predictable response, can, with re-training, be sent to a completely different nerve, producing a completely different response.

Neuroplastic Change

It does this through a process called Neuroplasticity[6]. Despite its complicated name, it is simple to understand, and explains so much of why we get stuck, and what we need to do to get unstuck.

First, let's break this word down into its two components. Neuro - meaning something to do with our nervous system, which we explored earlier; and plastic - meaning something that can change shape and grow.

If we imagine a signal being sent down this nerve, labelled '1'. It gets to a point where the nerve ends. This gap between the nerves is called a synapse. At this point, there are several different pathways this signal could go down. Let's imagine the one labelled '2' goes towards stress and the one labelled '3' goes towards relaxation.

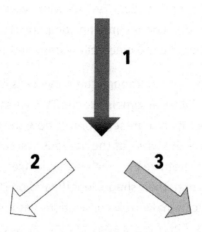

When the signal reaches the end of the nerve, it triggers the release of chemicals, called neurotransmitters, into the gap between the nerves. These neurotransmitters move across the gap and will cause one of the nerves on the other side of the gap to get excited enough to fire off a new electrical signal that travels onward down that nerve. If nerve 2 is the one that gets excited, it will produce the experience of stress. If we keep stimulating this nerve that produces stress, then neuroplasticity kicks in. It's the way the brain learns. It recognises that this pathway between nerve 1 and nerve 2 is being used quite regularly, so it helps this connection to be faster by moving nerve 2 closer to 1 and nerve 3 farther away.

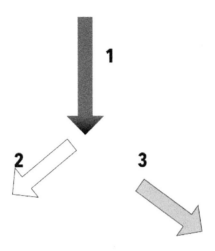

The effect of this is that the next time a signal comes down nerve 1 it's going to be much easier for it to jump across to nerve 2 (producing stress) than to go all the way to nerve 3 (producing relaxation). From this, it seems like neuroplasticity is troublesome for us because now it's helped us learn how to experience stress more effectively. But that's not entirely true. It's important to realise that neuroplasticity is just a process. It's not concerned with whether what it's learning is good or bad. It just recognises which nerves are being used the most and moves them closer together, while the least used ones are moved further apart. If we decide to push the signal to the less used one, 3, which is a bit trickier as it's further away, things start to change.

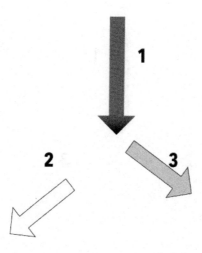

As we keep firing nerve 3 then, through the same neuroplastic process, it now moves closer to 1 and nerve 2 moves further away. As a result, it becomes easier for us to feel calm and relaxed because that pathway now has a much smaller gap than the one that triggers stress. And this is how change occurs. Each time we pause the limiting pathways that we've got used to and make a choice to move into a pathway that is less familiar, but probably more useful for us, then life gets a bit better. Even more importantly, each time we make this choice, we are training our brain to know this is the pathway we want to use. After a little time, this pathway will become our new go-to response. This is why neuroplasticity is so important. It helps us understand how we can:

- Stay stuck and not change.
- Fall into bad habits.
- Change some things and not others.
- Make change that's rapid and lasting, even in things that have been stuck for a long time.

Keep the concept of neuroplasticity in the forefront of your mind throughout this book. It's behind everything we'll cover. It's a huge topic, but to summarise the key takeaways are:

1. Your brain will become better at whatever you do most frequently, good or bad, due to the practice you're giving it. This includes piano practice, sports abilities, chess, arguments, stress, pain, self-doubt, etc.
2. Getting into a bad mood affects us in two ways.
   a. It feels bad and makes life suck.
   b. Probably even more importantly, it trains our brains making it even easier to feel bad in the future.
3. Luckily the same applies for good moods too. Getting into a good mood:
   a. Feels good and improves life.
   b. Trains our brains making it even easier to feel good in the future.
4. Neuroplasticity is ALWAYS on - so change is always possible.

In the next few chapters, you're going to learn how to practically apply this. You'll explore some common issues that many find themselves stuck with. Once you've understood how much the brain can change, you'll realise how it's possible to change these issues too, and this is important because getting free of them is a central part of developing your IW. Your next stop on our journey into IW is considering the life-changing topic of States.

'Neuroplasticity Is ALWAYS On - So Change Is Always Possible.'

CHAPTER 3: BEST STATE

WHAT IS A STATE?

A vital component of IW is an understanding of 'states'. Throughout the book, 'states' is used to mean 'wherever your mind and brain are focused right now'. Other ways to think of it are:

- Your state of mind.
- Your mood.
- What kind of mental processing you are doing.
- Which parts of your neurology you are using.
- The emotions you are experiencing.
- Where your attention is focused.

Here's a list of some familiar states, but, as you can sense from the list there are hundreds of them:

- Angry.
- Happy.
- Sad.
- Confident.
- Excited.
- Creative.
- Motivated.
- Stressed.
- On high alert.
- Relaxed.
- Thoughtful.
- Meditative.
- Focused.

As you read this book you may be:

- **Fascinated** by what you're reading.
- **Focused** on the content.
- **Remembering how angry** you've been with a friend recently.

- **Distracted**, and skipping to what you might be having for dinner.
- **Imagining** where I was when I was writing this.

All these are examples of being in different states, which will produce different feelings and result in different actions, responses, and decisions. For example, if someone is **fascinated,** they'll continue reading and get the best from the experience. If they're **remembering how angry** they were with a friend, much of their focus will be on that and less on the book's content. They may then put the book down, stew in their anger, write them an angry email or call them to resolve it. As we can see from this list, we are **always** in one state or another all the time - apart from, possibly, when asleep or unconscious. Even being at peace, in flow, meditation, and going blank, are all states. And from all these examples above we can notice that there are two essential issues to grasp about the nature of humans and states.

Two Issues We Have With States

First, ask yourself, 'Are people generally in the most useful state for the situation that they are in?'

If they're at work, are they focused on it or distracted? If they're in a meeting are they present or waiting for it to end? If they're doing household chores, are they pleased they have a house to clean or hurrying to finish this tiresome task? If they're watching a film, are they fully engaged with it or wondering what they'll do later? If they are relaxing on a sunny day, are they relaxing rather than thinking about what jobs they haven't done? It's clear from this, that many of us, much of the time, are not in the most useful state for the job that we are currently doing.

The classic example of this is when we're late for a plane and find ourselves in a slow-moving traffic jam, which means we might miss our flight. What state do we slip into? Often, it's stress, frustration, or anger. But if we ask this question, 'Is this the most useful state?', the answer is clearly no. The consequences of getting into these states are that we are more likely to make rash decisions, take a 'shortcut' which turns out to not be one, stall or crash the car, or have an argument with the person we're in the car with (maybe not the ideal start to your holiday). We can also notice that being in these states does not help: the speed of the car through the traffic, being on time, or starting the trip in the best possible mood. So, we've picked a state that is not helpful, worsens the situation, and feels bad. And yet this, or something similar, is an experience that most of us have had at some point.

So, the answer to that first question is, 'No. Most of the time we are not in the best, most optimal state for the job that we're doing'.

The second issue we have is that, even if we are aware of our non-optimal state (and we often aren't), most of us have very few effective strategies for being able to shift into a better one. They are usually limited to, taking some mind-altering substance (e.g., coffee, alcohol, drugs), turning up the music so it's loud, escaping the situation, or taking it out on something/someone (e.g., punching the wall, cursing the traffic, weather, partner, etc.). Although some of these help us switch from one state to another with varying degrees of success, most have side effects that we may not want, and sometimes may just not be practical in some situations. It's difficult to run away when you're driving a car in traffic, or to listen to loud music when you're in an interview. So, learning how to change your state without relying on these external methods is a core skill of IW, but how do we do that? How many people say to themselves, 'I wish I could spend a little bit more time just being present to the wonder of being alive, the birds in the sky, the beauty of the flowers, and how good it feels to be here.' Interestingly, being in a traffic jam is probably an ideal time to get into that state of deep calm presence and gratitude for being alive. And yet, how many people are able to do that in a traffic jam? Very few. What if we could do that - switch from one state to another at will, anywhere, anytime? How much easier would that make life? The answer is probably 'much easier' because being in the wrong state seems to make everything more difficult. When you look at your life, you can probably see that at the times when it worked best, you were in a great state.

And when things didn't quite work out well, it was a combination of what was happening and your response - the state that you were in - that made it more difficult to deal with. In this book, we will be looking at exactly how you make these kinds of shifts. It is one of the most important things you could ever learn to do, and one that is not part of most people's education or current skill set. Over the course of the book, you will master a range of state-shifting skills.

CHECK-IN
There are two important takeaways about states in the section above:

1. We are often in the wrong state - so we need to increase our awareness of this in order to change it, by asking ourselves, 'Am I in the best state for this moment?' So much of the time, the answer to this is 'No' which makes life much harder for us.
2. As we can also get stuck in those states, skills to shift out of them rapidly and effectively would be useful.

If you were to reflect on the last 14 days, what percentage of the time have you been in the best possible state for the job that you were doing? If you were with the kids, were you really with them? If you were eating your food, did you really focus on your food and not on your phone, or that you had to do the washing up later, etc.? And treat this like a yes or no question, being in a mediocre state that 'Wasn't too bad' or was 'Ok' means you weren't in the best state for that moment. What's your percentage? I've found most people find they're in the best state about 20% of the time - if your score is higher than that, you're already ahead of the game. But even if you're in the best state 50-60% of the time, that still means there's a huge chunk of time when you're not in the state that you want to be in, where life becomes more difficult. Even worse, because of neuroplasticity, each time you access a state that isn't that useful, it becomes easier to get into it again in the future. However, the same applies to good states. This means there's a double payoff to finding your way into the best state for the situation. Not only does it feel better and make life easier, but it also becomes easier to get into that state again in the future.

WORDS, STATES AND NEUROPLASTICITY

Words are interpreted very literally by the brain. My dog knows the word 'walk'. When I say, 'It's time for a walk', she gets very excited, runs around in a circle, looks for her lead, and knows that she's going out for a doggy adventure. But what happens if I say, 'You can't go for a walk right now because I'm busy writing a book'? She hears the word 'Walk' and has the same excited response as if we're going on a walk immediately. This teaches us something very important about how the brain processes negatives. It doesn't do a very good job of it. You may have had the experience of placing your credit card into a card reader and, while it's processing, it helpfully reminds you, 'Do not remove the card'. A fair amount of the time, we will remove the card because we've seen the word 'remove'. When working with a group of pain consultants, I was intrigued to see what their vocabulary was like. I asked them what they wanted for their clients and to avoid using or referring to the word 'pain' in their answers. (I'll stop using that word now and replace it with this symbol @) They took some time and struggled to come up with a suitable answer. Most proposed 'no @', 'lack of @' or '@-free'. Their best suggestion, which didn't include the word @, was 'relief'. But of course, the word relief means 'relief from @'. Unfortunately, each time you say, or think about, the word @ it wakes up and fires the pathways related to @ experience[7], this one isn't a great answer either. The same is true of the words stress, anger, hit, worry, etc. When we say to a child, 'Don't hit him' the first thing that comes to their mind is 'hitting him'. The words 'There's nothing to be worried about' immediately make our brain think about what we should be worried about, and so on. Our brain processes the words, 'Walk' and 'No walk', 'Remove' and 'Do not remove', '@' or 'no @' by firing off the same pathway for each pair. If you are a patient with @, then your experience of that @, and neuroplasticity, will, unfortunately, result in those pathways being built so they are fast and strong. Our @ specialist unwittingly deepening this process is something we don't need, and luckily, it can be easy for them to change, once they realise how much their words matter. The same is true for us as patients. Becoming aware of which words we are using and making sure they are building the pathways we want to build makes us a powerful force in our journey to wellness.

Word Exercise
Have a look at the following list of words and replace each negative one with a positive. You may find it interesting, as many people struggle with this task. This is a sign of how much neurology has been built that leads us into the pathways of 'trouble, symptoms, and problems'. Remember, there can be no blame or fault attached to this - this is just an effect of neuroplasticity. The more your brain uses negative words, the better it will become at it. Equally, the more you train your brain in this new 'what I want' direction, which will be a bit clunky to start with, the better you'll become at that too.

Word list

Use this first example as a guide:

'I want to not be stressed.'

becomes...

'I want to be calm.'

Here are some for you to work through. Write down your answers first - there's a list of potential answers on the next page:

1. I want no pain in my leg.
2. I want to be free of guilt.
3. I don't want to be stiff.
4. I don't want to be angry.
5. I want to be unstressed.
6. I want to stop feeling stupid.
7. I want to be unembarrassed.
8. I want to be non-judgemental.
9. I don't want to be constantly complaining.
10. I want to not be ill.

11. I don't want to be a perfectionist.
12. I don't want to get drunk.
13. I don't want to break my diet.
14. I want to stop procrastinating.

Here are some possible answers:

1. I want no pain.
    a. I want a deeply comfortable leg.
2. I want to be free of guilt.
    a. I want to be at peace with my decisions.
3. I don't want to be stiff.
    a. I want to be supple and flexible.
4. I don't want to be angry.
    a. I want to be thoughtful and choose my responses.
5. I want to be unstressed.
    a. I want to be profoundly calm.
6. I want to stop feeling stupid.
    a. I want to get in touch with and value my IW.
7. I want to be unembarrassed.
    a. I want to feel good about who I am and what I choose to do.
8. I want to be non-judgemental.
    a. I want to be totally accepting of myself and others.
9. I don't want to be constantly complaining.
    a. I want to see the good in things.
10. I want to not be ill.
    a. I want to be vibrantly well.
11. I don't want to be a perfectionist.
    a. I want to do my best and know it is enough.
12. I don't want to get drunk.
    a. I want to choose wisely so I'm completely happy with how I feel afterwards.
13. I don't want to break my diet.
    a. I want to eat in a healthy and balanced way.
14. I want to stop procrastinating.
    a. I want to be motivated, start, and follow through on my plan.

Hidden Negatives
There is a special class of words that appear at first to be positive but contain a hidden negative. The first type is called an 'away from' as in 'I

want to feel relief'. Notice there is a silent 'from' in this sentence, which probably ends with 'I want to feel relief from this pain'. As we learned earlier, this unfortunately re-stimulates and further strengthens the pathways of pain[8] as 'away from' type statements like these have the same effect as 'I do not want this' ones. The second common type is the words 'safe, secure, or protected' or 'brave, strong, bold, or courageous'. These words again seem like they're positive, but we would only need to be safe, secure, or protected, or, brave, strong, bold, or courageous, when we were facing some kind of danger or threat. So, using these words refocuses our brains on our concerns about the danger. From what we've learned about neuroplasticity, the more we think about danger, the more stressed we feel, and the more skilled we become at seeing potential dangers everywhere. Whenever you find yourself saying these words, turn them into true positives by asking, 'If I had that, what would that give me?'. For example: 'If I had safety, what would that give me?' The answer might be, 'I'd feel like I could try out new things.' Or: 'If I was courageous, what would that give me?' The answer might be, 'The confidence to move forward'. The third type is the word 'Control', as in, 'I want to control my anger'. This is a common way of expressing some positive change that you desire. But the word 'control' is applied to things that are, by their very nature, chaotic and unpredictable and have the potential to become dangerous. We can notice this from its use in these phrases 'drug control, border control, infection control, gun control, crowd control etc.'. Notice how strange it would sound to hear someone describe their holiday with any of the above words:

- 'It was controlled...'
- 'It was safe...'
- 'I was courageous...'
- 'I was relieved by how it was...'

These phrases don't suggest a very calm and relaxing holiday environment.

Also, notice how just swapping the word 'control' for 'choice' completely changes things.

- 'I want to control what I eat.' - 'I want to choose what I eat.'
- 'I want to control how I respond to them.' - 'I want to choose how I respond to them.'

Keep these sneaky hidden negatives in mind when choosing your words and goals. We'll also revisit them in the IWT 17 on dealing with inner conflict.

WORDS AND OTHER PEOPLE

With this new understanding of the power of words, we can sometimes be tempted to help others by alerting them to their use of negative language. Assisting others in this way raises some interesting points that are worth considering. Firstly, as you may have found from personal experience, we rarely like receiving unsolicited advice, and we often don't take it well or act on it, even if it's well-meant and incredibly valuable. As a result, it's generally wisest to avoid this kind of interaction. Pointing out their use of negatives, without being asked, naturally falls into this category. Secondly, to build great relationships with other people, it's vital that they feel heard and understood and that they have a sense of connection with you. Correcting their use of negative words can easily break any sense of connection that you have with them. And without this sense of connection, you won't be able to help them at all. For this reason, even though words have such power, it's so important to let people speak, vent, and express what's going on for them, as much as they need to, without any correction from anybody else. Once they feel heard and understood, you can, if appropriate, gently move on to discussing the value of language, but maintaining that sense of connection is always more important than getting the words right. We will be covering a range of skills on how to deal with other people in Chapter 21.

Key Takeaways

These concepts are so important to IW that we'll come back to them many times, but as an overview for easy reference:

1. Awareness - We need to be mindful of the state we are in.
2. Change - We need to notice if we are in the wrong state and use all the tools in the book to change our state. I promise it will make life so much easier and better for you and everybody else concerned.
3. Training - We need to remember the power of neuroplasticity - that the more we access a state, the easier it becomes to get into it. This is why if we've been angry all day, it's so much easier to become irritated at the smallest incident later on in the evening.
4. Words - We need to remember that our words trigger states, and so use them wisely, with ourselves and others, especially when we're talking about what we want.
5. Connection - When thinking about using these ideas with others, pause and make sure you're always keeping that sense of connection and sensitivity towards their needs.

This may seem like a simple set of ideas, but they are life-changing. I've seen people get out of wheelchairs, stop years of drug use, resolve their depression, and turn their lives around just by applying these essential pieces of IW and connecting with 'The Coach That's Always There'.

With these essential components of IW on board, we're ready to move onto the exciting world of Gateway States.

'We Need To Be Mindful Of The State We Are In.'

CHAPTER 4: GATEWAY STATES

Now we understand how vital states are in developing IW and having an easier and better life, let's introduce Gateway States.

USEFUL STATES

In my clinical work, I often find people need to switch into one of the following groups of states to move life forward:

A. Calmness, relaxation, or inner peace.
B. Confidence, a sense of competence, or thinking rationally.
C. Motivation, creativity, or inspiration.
D. A sense of humour, the ability to get perspective or to gain some distance.

If someone is, for example, angry or stressed they probably need to get in touch with the states listed in A. If they are doubting themselves or nervous before a presentation or interview, they probably also need those from B. The states in C are great to resolve procrastination around a new project or when running out of steam in a current adventure and those in D are valuable in so many places, great for seeing things differently, not taking things so seriously, regrouping and moving forwards. There are other states that people can need, but these four groups are very often the missing ingredients to make change. They're awesome... but these are not the Gateway States. Gateway States take change to a new level.

GATEWAY STATES

I started noticing Gateway States when working with people who had experienced something almost magical within the process of change. Accessing these Gateway States seemed to transform what happened next. They rewrote the book on how easy change was and how they felt about themselves and their future, and often, it redrew their understanding of their world. It was almost as though these states were catalysts for change, like rocket fuel or a wormhole that provided a passage to transport them from one phase of their life to another, almost instantly. Let's list these Gateway States, these agents of transformational change, as a starting point. The rest of the book will deepen your understanding of what is meant by each Gateway State in this list, and how to use it in a range of powerful IWT. The Gateways States are:

1. TRUST.

2. INNER COACH.

3. KINDNESS AND COMPASSION.

4. CURIOSITY.

5. SHIFT.

6. TRANSFORMATION.

7. CONNECTION.

This list is a useful start, but you might be asking, 'What are they and how do you use them?' Let's dive further into each one, learn how to get in touch with them, explore how they can change your worldview, and discover the IWTs that use them to create powerful change.

'Gateway States Take Change To A New Level.'

CHAPTER 5: TRUST

TRUST

When I was searching for solutions for my injured hand, you may recall that I came up against a depressing set of expert opinions about the hopelessness of recovery. Let's break down how I processed this in a bit more detail to get a glimpse of our first Gateway State. I think three major things show up:

- You can sense the difference of opinion between what others, in this case, the experts, were saying, 'You will never recover', and my sense that 'There has to be a way'. I had to find my path through this flood of well-meaning but negative opinions that didn't fit with my own.
- I think that holding onto my own perspective during this difficult time, was important. It helped me question their experience-driven, yet limiting, opinions about my future - at least until I had exhausted all possibilities. I'm certain this allowed me to continue asking and searching for some glimmer of possibility, despite the setbacks and negative prognoses.
- You can also sense that I decided to hold off adopting the opinions of the experts, and adding them to my inner dialogue, until I had more information.

These kinds of ways of dealing with the stuff of life show up the presence of our first Gateway State 'Trust' and as we'll see throughout the book, it's a state that can be useful in many situations. It's a central part of re-discovering 'The Coach That's Always There' and refers to that ability to listen to your IW, your inner voice, your truth, and to trust yourself, knowing that you know more about yourself, your dreams, your desires, and what motivates you than anybody else does. This sense of deep Trust in ourselves is often combined with a sense of knowing that things are unfolding in the way they should and that we can sense some bigger plan at work. When we get in touch with this Trust it allows for a deeper sense of our potential for change. Our direction forward becomes clearer. It connects us with what we know is deeply important, and our big life goals and sense of purpose, or 'mission' become clearer (more on this Chapter 21). Trust allows this 'mission' to become our guide to all that we do, and obstacles feel like they are just part of the journey rather than being a dead end or a full stop. This makes the future feel like something we can flow and dance through because we have a constant centre, a solid certain place to come from. It means that it doesn't matter how things shift and change around us, whether the path to our goal is straight or winding, we know when we are connected to Trust, that there will be a way and we will find it.

YOU'RE THE EXPERT ON YOU

The perspective of valuing your own opinion, rather than relying entirely on those of others, is central to IW and the concept of 'The Coach That's Always There'. It is summarised by the intriguing idea that 'no one could ever know you as well as you know yourself'. That you are the expert on 'being you'. This differs from many models, where others are considered to have better insight into you and your issues than you could have. Although in certain contexts, for example, in some aspects of medicine or car mechanics, this may well be true and valuable, elsewhere it is less helpful. In some earlier forms of psychotherapy, for example, the therapist was considered to be able to understand you and your motivations better than you. This prevailing model was later challenged by many, including one visionary therapist, Carl Rogers. He felt working collaboratively with the client as an equal, drawing on their expertise based on their life experience and desires might be more valuable than interpreting and assuming such things from the 'outside'. And when you think about it, isn't it true that you know your true strengths, likes, and goals, as well as the ways you can trick, trip, or undermine yourself, better than anyone else does? Recognising this opens up some interesting ideas. What if we could tap into this deep knowledge of ourselves, both in terms of our strengths and the way we undermine ourselves, as a route for change? Having direct access to this would make it simpler to know what we needed to avoid to stop getting ourselves into trouble and what skills we had at our fingertips to make life easier. This, then, is the first step to building IW and developing your connection with 'The Coach That's Always There', by realising that you do know yourself better than anybody else. That your dreams, desires, skills, experiences, and the things you want and like are more known to you than anybody else in the world. The next step then is to tap into that knowledge, using tools that we will cover as your journey through the book progresses.

SUPPORT AND ADVICE OF OTHERS

It's also important to recognise that just because you do know yourself better than anyone else, that does not mean you have to do it alone. You can, of course, get support, help, and guidance from others - there are times when their perspective and expertise will be essential. But we need to choose whom we ask and what areas of our lives we ask them for help with. You don't want, for example, to rely on others' opinions about your life, choices, decisions, or actions. They simply do not have the same level of information and knowledge required to answer those questions as you do. For example, imagine Sam asks you the question, 'Should I marry Jo?'. You know that this is a question that only Sam could possibly answer. Everybody else may have an opinion, they may have external observations and experience of the two together, but they don't have the direct experience that Sam has; and, of course, they won't be the ones marrying and spending their lives with Jo as a result of the answer. Hopefully, if you were Sam, you wouldn't ask this question, although it is one I have been asked many times in the course of my career; and if you were Sam's friend, you wouldn't feel it was yours to answer either. But many people fall into this pattern of asking others about things concerning their lives that they, rather than the friend, are best placed to answer. If you tend to ask advice from people who could never have as much insight into your life and this situation as you do, then you'll find the later sections covering some techniques to resolve this valuable. They will help you shift this back to where it should be, on trusting your own opinions and judgement about things that you are the expert on. Now let's apply these important concepts in the first IWT.

IWT 1: Reconnect With The Spark

Set aside 5 minutes for this first technique, which will reconnect you to some powerful moments in your past. Find a place where you can focus without being disturbed. Sit or stand and take 5 deep, easy breaths to get yourself ready to follow the steps. You might want to record these steps on your phone, with pauses in between each step, and play them back as a guide to help you through the process. I have created an audio series to accompany this book, which you might find helpful. It guides you through each step of the interactive IWTs, so that you can put the book down while focusing on following the processes. The guides to two IWTs that I recommend you use daily, this one 1 and 'Calm' IWT 6, are available for free here: philparker.org/IW. You can also purchase and download the full audio for the other interactive IWTs there.

1. Allow your mind to drift back through the thousands of memories that you've collected throughout your life, to a time when you had a deep sense of Trusting yourself. Many types of moments may stand out for you. The common examples that follow may help you choose one:
    a. You may recall a time when you were making a decision, such as buying a house or moving to a new apartment, choosing a new job, or relocating to a new city, and felt this house/job/city felt just right...Or maybe you felt that sense of knowing that 'Yes, this is the right one', or, 'No, this isn't the right one for me'.
    b. You may recall a time when someone else suggested or made a choice for you that you just knew was a bad fit for you. Independent of whether you fought against them or went along with it anyway, focus on that sense of 'knowing this isn't right for me'.
    c. You may recall a time when someone in authority told you very clearly that 'this is something you won't ever be able to achieve because you're too slow/clumsy/stupid/short/tall, etc. and you felt that push-back inside of you that said, 'NO! You don't know

what I can achieve, and now you've made me even more committed to doing it'.

   d. You may recall a time when you had the sense that you knew that what you were doing and where you were heading was part of the plan, the right direction for you. And, although you weren't certain of the precise details, of what would happen next, things would work themselves out.

   e. You may recall a time when you knew that what you were doing was such an important part of your life - getting a sense of what you could contribute to others; connecting with the bigger picture of where you were heading; feeling the unique contribution you could make to something you knew to be important; having that strong sense of 'mission' and purpose.

   f. You may be inspired by hearing about someone else's journey and connect with how they tuned into their sense of trusting themselves, even when there was some resistance to their vision.

2. Whichever one you choose, fully connect with it, and immerse yourself in that experience. As you step fully into it, notice what you can:

   a. **See** around you.

   b. **Hear** what's going on around you as well as what's going on inside your head.

   c. **Feel** physically (such as your breathing and posture, the temperature on your skin, etc.) and emotionally.

3. If that feeling and sensation were to have a colour, what colour would it be? Let that colour flow throughout your body, becoming even stronger and deeper with each breath.

Notice how great it feels to just recall these powerful moments from your past. I'd recommend revisiting this IWT daily. Doing this, switches on the pathways of these 'Trust' memories, releasing a range of neurochemicals and hormones throughout your body. And, because of neuroplasticity, the more you practice this, the easier you'll find it to get in touch with these memories. As you connect with this 'Trust' ask yourself, 'Where in the next few days or weeks would it be useful to re-access this feeling?'

We will revisit this IWT as a starting point for many of the other techniques.

'No One Could Ever Know You As Well As You Know Yourself.'

CHAPTER 6: INNER COACH

The second Gateway State in IW is 'Inner Coach' and is alluded to in the book's title. It is less familiar than the concept of Trust for many, so we will take a little time to introduce it and the field of 'coaching'. On that journey, we'll explore what a coach is, what they do, what qualities they need to be effective and how you can develop the life-changing skills of Inner Coaching.

COACHING

Coaching as a way of creating change gained traction in the 1980s. It's an approach that supports people to steer their lives in a new direction and is centred around the concept introduced in the last chapter that you 'know yourself better than anyone else could'. The origin of the word 'coach' helps our understanding of what good coaching can achieve. In the 1500s, the bumpy country roads between the fabulous cities of Vienna and Budapest made travel uncomfortable for those making the journey. Word spread of how the superior design of the carriages made in the town of Kocs, Hungary, transformed the journey, allowing people to travel in style and comfort. Over time the word 'Kocsi' (the carriages from Kocs) transformed into 'coaches'. So, in transport, a coach is something that helps you find your way over difficult terrain in the easiest way possible; in terms of coaching people, a coach helps them find the easiest way through the challenges and opportunities of life. There's another definition I think is particularly helpful, which is: 'Coaching is an empowering conversation that inspires you to design a life that you love'. There are so many important parts to this definition that it's valuable to break it down piece by piece. First, it identifies that coaching is delivered primarily through conversations. But it's not chatting, it's a conversation that is empowering and that leaves you feeling even more powerful, influential, and competent to steer your life where you wish it to go than before. Second, it includes the idea that you will 'design' a 'life you love'. It's clear from this that the coach will not be telling or instructing you what to do. Instead, they will be inspiring you so that YOU can create and build your future life.

The word 'Inspire' comes from the Latin (in spirare) to 'breathe into' and originally conveyed the sense that life force or spirit (which comes from the same word) would be breathed into the person. This sense lead to its modern meaning of encouraging and moving someone to take action. Note, also, how active your role as the person being coached (or coachee) is here. The coachee is going to be taking on the job of designing that life because, of course, they, not the coach, are the expert on 'them'. Finally, the life you are designing is identified very specifically, not just as an 'OK' life, or a 'good' life, but as a 'life you love', so something pretty awesome. This statement emphasises that it is possible to have a great life through design, and that through the simple but powerful art of conversation, delivered within a coaching context, that this is achievable. A great coach can do an amazing job of helping you find the quickest and most effective route to achieving your goals. As explained above, the process relies on your input, expertise, and engagement to help shape and create solutions to the problems that you find yourself with. The coach's job is to help you focus your thoughts and plans in a useful way. There are some other skills of coaching, that we'll come to later, but these are the fundamentals. So how does a coach help that change process, and how is this linked to IW?

INNER COACH

From above, we can see that in coaching, the coach assists the coachee to get busy working on the problems from the inside, to provide solutions. So, would it also be possible to create an Inner Coach, so we can take on that coaching role to assist 'us', in a similar way to find those solutions? Rather excitingly, the answer is 'Yes' and this is something you'll be building through the Gateway State and the IWT of Inner Coach. This is partly the inspiration for the book's title, as in the sections that follow, you'll discover how you can physically take on the role of the Inner Coach to directly connect with, listen to and interact with your IW. Being able to tap into your IW in this extraordinary way is one of the most powerful skill-sets available. I've worked with people who've used it to resolve old anger, stress, depression, and confidence patterns, resolve physical symptoms, stop addictions and old habits, achieve goals, perform at their best, deal with criticism, respond to obstacles and unexpected events in a powerful way, and so much more.

COACHING QUALITIES

To develop and use the Gateway State of Inner Coaching we need to discover the qualities of a great coach, and you may be surprised to find that you already know quite a lot about this subject. Let's begin by using the powerful 3 Coaches exercise.

3 COACHES EXERCISE

Coaches can show up at important points in our lives. They take on a role where they are required to be supportive, to help and guide us through whatever we are dealing with.

We're going to look at three specific people from your past, who took on the role when you needed some coaching support in some aspect of your life. Coaches can come in many different flavours, and it may be that you didn't select them to be your coach by choice. They might have been a teacher, sports coach, parent, boss or friend - someone who was there to help you - but they may not have had any formal training or professional qualifications in coaching.

Keeping that in mind, I'd like you to pick the following three people from your past who took on that coaching role.

1. Great Coach

The first person you'll select is somebody whose job was to be your coach, and they were brilliant at it. Being around them helped you realise your potential and find your way through difficult times. Their presence helped move things on and it felt good to have them on your team. Write their name down and begin to list the qualities or skills you felt they had that made them so useful for you as a coach. Take a few minutes with this before moving on to part 2.

2. Poor Coach

The second person I'd like you to choose is someone who was given the role of being your coach. But in this case, they were awful. Being with them didn't feel like a good experience, it didn't seem to move things on and quite often made things worse. Write their name down and make a list of the qualities that made this such a difficult experience. Also, write down what qualities they were missing.

3. You As A Coach

Finally, I'd like you to choose a time in your life when you coached somebody effectively. This is a time when you were there for somebody, you supported them and helped them through a difficult time or challenge, and it was really valuable for them. Maybe you know this because, at some point, they told you that your being there in that way really helped them. Reflect on this time and write down what qualities you brought to that situation that made it a good experience for the person you were helping.

Now we can start to build the template for what makes a great coach.

1. Take the qualities:
    a. Present in your great coach.
    b. Missing and needed in the poor coach.
    c. Demonstrated by you when coaching someone else.
2. And combine them.

This powerful mix provides the most important qualities that are essential for great coaching.

Now that you've done this exercise, take a few minutes to check out the full list of coaching qualities I've included in the appendix. After you've done that, come back to the next section.

COACHING QUALITIES FOR INNER COACHING

It's quite a long list, but as you read it, you probably realised just how much you already knew about coaching. You would have identified many of the key qualities in the 3 coaches exercise. All of these can be useful for Inner Coaching, but these five are especially important for developing your IW:

1. Questions.
2. Perspective.
3. Flexible.
4. Humour/Lightness.
5. Kindness.

In the next few chapters, we'll be exploring these five qualities and applying them within some important IWT.

'Use Your Knowledge Of Yourself To Be Your Own Inner Coach.'

CHAPTER 7: INNER COACH - QUESTIONS AND PERSPECTIVE

QUESTIONS

The skill of asking questions instead of giving advice is core to coaching. This follows from the first IW concept we explored, the idea that you know yourself better than anybody else. Therefore, great coaching helps the client discover their own solutions rather than telling them what they need to do. And that is why questions are so important and so much more valuable than external advice. It also means that if you have a good understanding of the right kind of questions to ask, and we will be covering them, then you can quite easily take on the role of an effective Inner Coach. In the earlier section on negative words (Chapter 3), we explored how giving unasked-for advice can cause issues. Using wise questions can help us out here too. For example, imagine someone asks for your help because they get upset when receiving feedback. You might want to give the advice, 'You need to be better at dealing with criticism' or 'You need to be more resilient and trust yourself more'. Even if this is accurate advice, it is less likely to be accepted and taken on than the question, 'What do you feel you could learn from how that felt?' or 'How would you like to respond to such feedback in the future?' Notice how these questions allow the coachee to come up with their own solutions, which will fit their needs best and leave them feeling empowered as they've created the solution 'by themselves'. From this, we can see that learning to pause our advice-giving and ask questions is a wise choice that will increase how helpful we can be to others. However, not all questions are wise, kind, or useful. Watch out for the types of questions that start with 'Why?', such as 'Why didn't you clean up the kitchen?'. We need to recognise that this type of 'why?' question isn't asked because we are interested in the answer, instead, it's a ploy to point the finger of blame at someone and is a great way to start arguments. It's wiser to stop asking these kinds of questions and replace them with a 'How can we resolve this?' type question. We'll be looking at these kinds of issues in the later sections on blame and dealing with others (Chapters 14 and 21). We'll be using some powerful questions in the next IWT and combining them with the skill of 'perspective'.

PERSPECTIVE

This coaching quality is the ability to maintain a bigger view of things and to see beyond the current obstacles and limitations. This can be such an important role to have as a coach because when you're in the thick of a problem, sometimes, it can be hard to see a way out and easy to feel hopeless. The coach's perspective reminds us:

- There is a path going forward, a solution, an end to these difficulties, and better times ahead.
- Of who you are.
- That you have dealt with similar difficulties and challenges in the past and overcome them.
- That you have a whole range of skills that are perfectly designed for dealing with these kinds of issues.
- That you're creative and unstoppable.
- That, in the greater scheme of things, this is a smaller issue than it actually feels at the moment.

These kinds of perspectives are often absent when we feel stuck, and having the coach remind us of them is a vital part of regrouping, picking ourselves up, and continuing onward[9].

This ability to shift your sense of perspective, therefore, is such an important skill to develop as an Inner Coach. Having this inspirational and empowering force of nature that resiliently reminds us, time and time again, that we can do this and that we are enough, is going to be such an important asset for you in building a great future.

It can be tough when we're trying to find our way through things and we're not surrounded by the kind of supportive people we need. Being able to provide this sense of support and partnership is again where the Inner Coach is so valuable, and, as your Inner Coach, they will always be there for you.

IWT 2: Inner Coaching & The 'Knowing Yourself' Question

This next technique combines several of the elements we've explored so far. You'll be re-connecting with the Gateway State of Trust, learning how to use your Inner Coach and applying the qualities of coaching. It will use a technique where you move from one place to another while coaching yourself (the instructions will explain exactly how to do this).

MOVEMENT

This movement of stepping physically into a different space at a slight distance from yourself may seem a bit odd the first time you do it. However, the research, and experience, show that the 'self-distancing' achieved by stepping out and looking back at ourselves, is incredibly valuable[10,11]. By 'stepping away from ourselves' it feels as if we've left the problem some distance behind us. This is why people use phrases like 'I just need to get this in perspective', 'It's too in my face at the moment to make sense of it', 'I need to step out for a moment', 'I need to see this from a distance'.

From this distanced position, we feel less overwhelmed by the issue and its emotions, which allows us to step more easily into the role of the Inner Coach.

TALKING LIKE A COACH

As the Inner Coach, we can start to create a new inner conversation. Again, researchers have found that talking to yourself in this way is a core skill of peak performers. They have also found that shifting positive phrases or questions that start with 'I', such as 'I can do this', or 'What do I need to do?' to ones that start with 'YOU' instead are even more effective. Statements like, 'YOU can do this' or asking questions such as, 'What do YOU need to do?' have a more positive impact on how we feel about ourselves and how we deal with stress[11]. Researchers think the use of 'you' makes it feel like there is somebody else involved in the conversation, and we tend to respond positively to the encouragement and input of other members of 'our tribe'.

You will find this reflected in the instructions, which will helpfully remind you to use these 'YOU' type statements and questions. You'll discover for yourself how these 'YOU' phrases seem to naturally be a better fit than the 'I' versions when coaching yourself, and experience just how powerful it feels to use this specific type of language.

You will also be speaking out loud to yourself. This may feel unusual too, but keep at it, as it's very important. The research into both top athletes and those wanting to solve emotional issues shows that speaking out loud to yourself again increases the sense that there is someone else with you, supporting you, and makes this conversation more powerful [11,12].

MEANING IT

It's also essential when taking on the role of Inner Coach that you genuinely mean what you say. So, if the steps ask you to say, 'You're doing really well' or 'I'm proud of what you've achieved' then you need to say it as though you really mean it. This is because a half-hearted or sarcastic coach in real life is probably worse than no coach at all. We are very tuned in to when people are saying one thing and their body posture, or voice tone, says something different. A classic example of this is at the end of a date when somebody says, 'Listen, I've had a lovely evening with you, you're a very nice person...' but you know from the way they've said it that the next word is going to be 'But...' Although the words themselves sound quite positive, you can tell that they're going to end with, 'But I'm not sure this is going anywhere.'

Take your first steps into Inner Coaching, following the simple instructions below and see how it helps you see things differently.

Start by taking an issue you are currently facing. For this first time, to make it as simple as possible, choose something that's not the biggest challenge in your life, but something you would like to resolve.

Find a place where you can focus without being disturbed, and, as before, you might want to record these steps on your phone, or use my audio guide to the steps available here: philparker.org/IW, if you'd like to experience the IWTs in that way. To avoid too much repetition, I'll just note this as 'Get Prepared' next time.

Make sure there is about 1 metre of space in front of you. Stand up and take 5 deep, easy breaths.

1. Start in the 'You' position (shown by the dotted-line circle with the arrow pointing to the RIGHT in the diagram) and reconnect with the Gateway State of Trust that you accessed in IWT 1. Let your mind drift back through the thousands of memories that you've collected throughout your life, to a time when you had a deep sense of Trusting yourself.
2. As you step fully into it, notice what you can:
    a. **See** around you.
    b. **Hear** what's going on around you as well as what's going on inside your head.
    c. **Feel** physically (your breathing and posture, the temperature on your skin) and emotionally.
3. If that feeling and sensation were to have a colour, what colour would it be? Let that colour flow throughout your body, becoming even stronger and deeper with each breath.
4. Using the diagram as a guide:

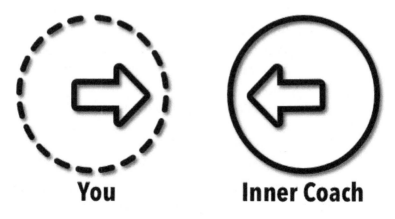

You   **Inner Coach**

a. From where you are now - the 'You' position (noted by the dotted-line circle with the arrow pointing to the RIGHT in the diagram).

b. Step into the space just in front of you (the solid-line circle) - marked 'Inner Coach'.

Then turn around 180 degrees so you are looking back towards the space you were just standing in (as shown by the arrow pointing to the LEFT).

5. In this solid-line circle, you will be taking the role of the Inner Coach.

a. First, imagine you can still see yourself standing in that dotted-line circle right in front of you - in the 'You' position. You don't have to actually see a complete 3D version of yourself, just imagining it will work perfectly. Stepping over to the Inner Coach position in this way provides that perspective we explored earlier that is so important in coaching.

b. The Inner Coach is going to direct all their questions and conversations to that 'You' over there in the dotted-line circle. As the Inner Coach, ask the following questions out loud.

6. Ask the 'You' over there:

a. Knowing yourself better than anybody else does.

b. Knowing your skills, abilities, and strengths.

c. And knowing the habits you have that can get in your own way (procrastination/self-doubt/getting overwhelmed/not saying 'No' when you should, etc.).

d. What do you need to focus on right now to move this issue forward?

7. Step back into the 'You' in the dotted-line circle and answer, out loud again, your Inner Coach's question.

8. Notice how powerful it feels to have had this conversation and gained these insights in this way.

Congratulations! You have taken your first steps in developing a profound relationship with your Inner Coach.

You've discovered how to step into your Inner Coach and start to use the qualities of coaching on yourself. These include stepping out of yourself and away from the problem so you can observe the issue from a distance. Notice how this simple use of movement is so important, as it physically separates us from the emotion of the issue and gives us that sense of perspective that is so valuable in helping us see things in a different light[10,13]. You can probably sense why recording it yourself or using the recordings I've made (for reference they are here: philparker.org/IW) might be of help in learning the IWTS.

You've used some valuable questions that will help you reconnect with the idea that you are the expert on you and will refocus you on working out what you need to do to resolve this problem.

We'll use many of these elements from this important technique and combine them with more of the elements of Inner Coaching that we will discover in the next few IWTs.

'Giving Advice And Sharing Our Wise Opinions Isn't An Effective Way To Help People.'

CHAPTER 8: INNER COACH - AWARENESS AND HUMOUR

FLEXIBLITY

There are so many ways of Inner Coaching depending on what you need in that moment. Sometimes a softer and more comforting approach is required; other times you'll need a firmer, more no-nonsense one; or to be inspired, listened to and heard, and so on. This flexibility to deliver the right kind of Inner Coaching relies on two factors. The first is developing 'awareness', which allows us to consider what is going to work best and check in with how it feels. I've found that many people are surprised at how they find themselves locked into coaching themselves in the same way that they've always talked to themselves. If that old style is harsh and unforgiving or tries to push them through their fears, they often find that switching the style of coaching to be kind and supportive can be life-changing. The second, is being 'outcome focused'. This is the Inner Coach's commitment to finding a way to get their coaching through to you, so 'You' can find a way to move forward. If your Inner Coaching isn't 'landing' as you hoped it would, then you keep changing it until it has the desired effect. When coaching others, this requires a high level of skill from the coach. They need to be observant, understanding, and intuitive of what their coachee requires from them at this moment. This is challenging as they have to estimate what is needed based only on what they can see, hear, and sense. However, in Inner Coaching this problem disappears because, of course, the Inner Coach has direct experience of what you're going through. This insight makes your Inner Coach a powerful ally because they already know what kind of coaching you need right now. This echoes the first concept of IW that 'you know yourself better than anybody else'. So, you will know when you need some time to pause and reflect, when you need firm coaching, when you need to be encouraged or supported, and so on. A professional coach can assess whether they've gauged their delivery correctly by asking themselves: 'Did it work?' 'Did the message I was trying to convey, and the support I intended, land effectively with my coachee?' 'Did it make a positive difference in the way I hoped and help them move on?' As an Inner Coach keep this idea in mind. Ask yourself, 'Did the kind of coaching I provided make the difference I needed?' If it didn't, consider mixing it up a bit and trying a different style of coaching, by asking yourself, 'What kind of coaching do I need right now?

IWT 3 Inner Coaching Style
Let's continue developing our IW by adding these elements to our Inner Coaching.

Start by thinking of something you're working through at the moment, a problem, obstacle, plan, project or goal. Again, at this early stage of learning the skills, choose something that's not the biggest challenge in your life, but something you would like to resolve.

Get prepared as before. Make sure there is about 1 metre of space in front of you. Stand in the 'You' position and take 5 deep, easy breaths. Just as a final reminder, the full audio guides for this and the other IWTs are available here philparker.org/IW, if you'd like to experience the IWTs in that way.

1. Start by reconnecting with that sense of Trust that you accessed in IWT 1.
2. As before, step into the space just in front of you (the solid-line circle) marked 'Inner Coach'. Then turn around 180 degrees so you are looking back towards the space you were just standing in (as shown by the arrow pointing to the LEFT). In this solid-line circle, you will be taking the role of the Inner Coach. See the 'You' still standing in that dotted-line circle right in front of you - in the 'You' position.

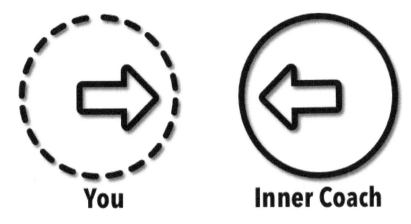

You   **Inner Coach**

3. Ask the 'You' over there, out loud:
    a. Knowing myself better than anybody else.
    b. Knowing the ways you can trip yourself up.
    c. Knowing the habits you have that can get in your own way.
    d. Knowing my skills, talents and expertise.
    e. What specific type (or style) of coaching would really work for you to help you move through this?
4. Now step back into the 'You' in the dotted-line circle and answer, out loud again, your Inner Coach's question.

Notice how, as a result of neuroplasticity, repeating some of the steps from the previous IWT makes using this one more familiar. This is a pattern you'll see throughout the book. With each IWT we'll be building on some elements you've used in previous ones, so by the end, you'll have a deep knowledge of these skills and find them easy to access.

HUMOUR AND LIGHTNESS

This often-undervalued quality is essential for great Inner Coaching, and it has much in common with the coaching quality of perspective. This is because bringing a sense of humour and lightness to a situation reduces how significant, difficult, or serious a thing feels. A key sign that we need to use our IWT is when we're losing our sense of humour. You may have observed this in yourself and others. Restoring our ability to see the funny side of a situation and take it less seriously is one of the first steps in regaining our perspective and regrouping. The importance of a sense of humour has been highlighted by many researchers. It has been studied in some of the most challenging environments such as working with terminally ill patients, where a compassionate use of a sense of humour by hospice staff was highly valued by patients [14]. We've already used humour in the IWT as we recognise that we have both incredible skills and the ability to get in our own way sometimes, and we will use it even more as we move forward. It is also seen to have great value in many spiritual traditions - in the Buddhist tradition, for example, Master Zhuang (c. 369 BC - c. 286 BC) wrote, 'To the most trivial actions, attach the devotion and mindfulness of a hundred monks. To matters of life and death, attach a sense of humour'[15] . Humour is a powerful ally in change but it must be used in combination with the final coaching quality, which is so important that it's also our next Gateway State, Kindness.

'To The Most Trivial Actions, Attach The Devotion And Mindfulness Of A Hundred Monks. To Matters Of Life And Death, Attach A Sense Of Humour.' - Master Zhuang

CHAPTER 9: KINDNESS AND COMPASSION

SELF-KINDNESS

This Gateway State and coaching quality, of being Kind to yourself is essential to our health, happiness, and success. It is often used to mean the same as self-compassion, although technically Self-Kindness is defined as one of the three elements of self-compassion (the other two being, first, a recognition of the shared human experience - realising that this is not just happening to me, but that we all go through difficult times - and second, mindfulness - being able to observe our emotions in an accepting way while not being swept away by them[3]). Developing Self-Kindness reduces our response to stress[16], which has many health consequences, including improving brain function, heart, digestive and immune system health and reducing addictions, habits and substance use [1,17–19].

Yet being Kind to ourselves is a skill that is deeply unfamiliar to many people. There is a question that I've used for many years that I think identifies this issue well. It is, 'If you treated your friends as you treat yourself, would you have any?'. For many people, the answer is no. If they spoke to other people in the same way they speak to themselves, their friends would run a mile, and they would probably lose their jobs for being rude and unpleasant towards their colleagues. So, if being hard on yourself is something you find yourself doing, or if you've been treating yourself with less Kindness than you would show to somebody that you care about, then maybe it's time to stop this old pattern. Fortunately, you'll find techniques throughout this book to do just that.

Imagine how much easier changing things will be when you can bring Self-Kindness to any errors, mistakes, or missteps you make as you find your path forward. What if you could bring Kindness to old unhelpful patterns you saw in yourself and in the reactions of others - how much would that help you?

Ram Dass, a Harvard psychologist and philosopher, had a nice take on this. He talked about trees in a forest and how, as they grew in an attempt to find the light they needed, some grew straight and some grew crookedly. When we're in the forest, we just enjoy the trees. We may notice the shapes and appreciate how much they've worked to get to the light. But he notes, we often don't do this with others or ourselves, instead, we judge it as 'Too this way or that'. He decided instead that it might be wiser to think of people as trees and appreciate them just the way they are.

Knowing you are enough just the way you are is a cornerstone of Self-Kindness and is another attribute that many of us could do with practising more.

Carl Rogers, the founder of the humanist approach to change, was demonstrating his technique to an audience. He began by explaining how he would work with a client and would detail everything that he was thinking that informed his therapeutic decisions as he went along. He told them his first step was to greet the client politely and kindly. Then he suddenly stopped and said to the audience that he had just realised something new, something that he always did, but had only just noticed. Before he even began to work or talk with a client, he always had a chat with himself. And in this conversation with himself, he reminded himself that, although he may not know everything about everything, he also knew that he was enough. And being enough, just being here, and bringing himself fully to this moment was all he needed to do to be of value and service to the client.

Keep these ideas in mind as you develop the role of being your Inner Coach and the quality of Self-Kindness. It is something you will use many times as it will form the bedrock of a number of other IWTs. There is some interesting research that describes how Self-Kindness is a two-way street. It identifies that when you are Kind to other people, it improves their well-being and health *and* also provides the same benefits to you as the giver of that Kindness[20]. This means that when you are using this approach in IWT and taking on the roles of Inner Coach and coachee, you will get twice the benefit - because you'll be both receiving and giving that Kindness.

IWT 4: Being Kind

Let's apply what we've learned so far and combine it with the idea of being Kind to yourself. Although this may appear, at first glance, to be a fairly simple technique, many people find they have a very powerful emotional response to it. This is due to the unfamiliarity many have with Self-Kindness and its health-promoting effects. Following these steps will get you in touch with being Kind to yourself in a profound way, and for many, that experience is unusual, lovely, and quite surprising.

Get prepared as before. Make sure there is about 1 metre of space in front of you. Stand in the 'You' position and take 5 deep, easy breaths.

1. Start by reconnecting with that sense of trusting yourself that you accessed in IWT 1.
2. Now reconnect with a memory of being Kind to yourself or someone else, in the same way, we connected with 'trusting yourself' in IWT 1. Allow your mind to drift back through the thousands of memories that you've collected throughout your life, to a time when you had a deep sense of Kindness. These common examples that follow may help you to choose one. Consider a time:
   a. When you recognised someone needed your support and Kindness, so you took the time to give that to them. It may have been a friend or family member in distress, an upset child, or a stranger who you knew needed some compassionate Kindness and care.
   b. When you came across an anxious animal who was stressed or ill and needed your support and Kindness, so you took the time to give that to them. Notice how it feels to be in touch with this Kindness you felt when you were with them.
   c. When you saw someone do something that was impressive or difficult for them to achieve, so you took the time to acknowledge them and let them know how much you admired what they had done.

d. When you noticed someone needed to be given Kindness, and attention and be heard, so you sat with them and really listened to them. You were able to empathise with them and understand the tough journey they had been on. You were able to listen without judgement and stay with them even though they were talking about difficult emotions. You were just there with them, letting them know you deeply cared about them and wanted to help in any way that they needed.

e. When you realised you needed to give Kindness to yourself, maybe you had been working hard for a long time and gave yourself a well-earned break. Maybe you realised you'd made an error or misstep and were able to let it go, realising you'd done your best. Maybe you recognised that you had achieved something important and took the time to recognise that.

f. You might want to step into the shoes of somebody who you think of as being incredibly Kind and compassionate. It may be someone you know personally or someone from history (such as the Buddha, Jesus, Mother Teresa, Martin Luther King, Jr., etc.).

3. As you step fully into whichever one you choose, notice what you can:
   a. **See** around you.
   b. **Hear** what's going on around you as well as what's going on inside your head.
   c. **Feel** physically (your breathing and posture, the temperature on your skin) and emotionally.

4. If that feeling and sensation were to have a colour, what colour would it be? Let that colour flow throughout your body, becoming even stronger and deeper with each breath.

5. As before:

a. From where you are now - the 'You' position
    (noted by the dotted-line circle with the arrow
    pointing to the RIGHT in the diagram).
b. Step into the space just in front of you (the solid-
    line circle)- marked 'Inner Coach'.
c. Then turn around 180 degrees so you are looking
    back towards the space you were just standing in
    (as shown by the arrow pointing to the LEFT).

You   **Inner Coach**

6. Looking directly at the 'You' over there, as the Inner
    Coach, say out loud and in a way that you know will get
    the message through to you:
    a. 'I'm so proud of you and all that you have
        achieved.'
    b. 'Like that time when you...' (List a few things that
        you know took a lot of effort from you to make
        happen).
    c. 'I see these qualities in you...' (List them)
    d. 'You're really good at...' (List a few stand-out
        examples of skills and abilities that you know you
        have. No one else is listening, so it's ok to say them
        out loud. Examples include being patient with
        kids/making fabulous soup/gardening/making
        friends, etc. but choose YOUR own).

e. 'And I really like that about you.'
f. 'I know you've had to deal with some stuff in your life and you always keep going.'
g. 'I know that like everyone else, although you don't always get it right all the time, you always do your very best.'
h. 'I think you are a truly amazing person.'
i. 'You (add your name), are enough'.
j. 'I love you.'

7. Step back into the 'You' in the dotted-line circle and feel how it feels to hear your Inner Coach say these things to you.

8. Let this in, then take some time to enjoy those feelings of Self-Kindness and acknowledgement. (If you find it less easy to let that in, then step back to the Inner Coach and keep on saying Kind things in as many different ways as you can until you finally get this message through.*)

9. Mentally take yourself into the future, where you've become great at this. Feel what it feels like to have this be a part of your everyday experience.

Notes:* It's so important to be Kind to ourselves, as it's linked to so many markers of good health. Despite that, many people discover they are deeply out of practice at self-Kindness. They've been told so many times over the years to not be nice to themselves, that they don't deserve it or that being Kind to yourself is arrogant or egotistical. But this is a misunderstanding of what Self-Kindness means. The Self-Kindness you're building here acknowledges that we're not perfect, that we all make errors from time to time AND recognises that we are worthy of love and Kindness anyway.

Step 6: Because Self-Kindness is so important you will see this set of compassionate, supportive, and affirming statements repeated in many of the IWT. It's vital, as mentioned before, to say these things and really mean them *each* time. If you find yourself getting tired of repeating the same words (I sometimes do), or if the phrases don't quite work for you, then get creative and come up with some other ways to say the same kind of things. Make each time feel like it's the most important time your Inner Coach has ever said it to 'You'.

Congratulations! You have taken a further step in creating a powerful Inner Coach.

You've added the additional skills of connecting with Kindness and being Kind to yourself. Being Kind is such an important component of IW and essential for making any change that's sustainable. You may need to return to this IWT a few times during the book. This is because occasionally, in the process of change, we might discover aspects of ourselves or behaviours that we don't like much. Although this can lead to self-criticism, it's actually an important signal reminding us that it's time to be Kinder to ourselves.

In step 9 you may have noticed we included the coaching qualities from the last chapter on flexibility.

This interesting combination of coaching qualities will help refine your Inner Coaching and help you to see things differently, which is a huge part of our next Gateway State, Curiosity.

Reflection
In these chapters on Trust and Inner Coaching, we've covered some important components of IW. We have:

- Discovered what is meant by IW and recognised that we are the expert on 'us'.
- Learned how to build and use our IW Inner Coach.
- Found how stepping physically between the Inner Coach and 'You' shows us the power of perspective and movement.
- Experienced the benefits of having a great Inner Coach. They:

- o Already have all the inside knowledge and insights about you, your issues, preferences, talents, etc. guiding the coaching process.
- o Know the best questions to ask you, and the best way to phrase a question to get your attention, as your Inner Coach is the world's leading expert on being you, after all.
- o Know the ways you can trip yourself up and avoid change, so know exactly what to do to help you stay on track with your goals.
- o Are always there, 24/7. Even when most coaches have gone home, your Inner Coach will be freely available at a moment's notice.
- Discovered the importance of Kindness

When we apply the qualities of great coaching to our Inner Coaching we can sense what a powerful resource this is. When we can learn how to access this, at any time, it means we can feel we have an inner ally supporting us, no matter what challenges arise. We will continue to develop your Inner Coaching even further as we explore the other Gateway States and IWTs.

Before we continue to the next section, I recommend pausing for a moment to list the most important and valuable things you've learnt from everything that we've covered so far.

'If You Treated Your Friends Like You Treat Yourself, Would You Have Any?'

CHAPTER 10: CURIOSITY

CURIOSITY

Our next Gateway State 'Curiosity', is one of my favourite states. It describes the state of mind we get into when we're intrigued by something new that we've come across. We've suspended our judgement about what we think we'll find, and we're open to whatever we discover. It's the opposite of having a fixed mindset where we feel we already know how everything is or have prejudged how something will be.

CURIOSITY AND STUCKNESS

Curiosity is particularly valuable when we find ourselves dealing with something unexpected that gets in the way of our plans. Quite often, we will respond to these unexpected events as failures or as evidence that something or someone has gone wrong. We may feel stuck, criticised, or that we've been made to look bad. This is where getting into the Gateway State of Curiosity provides such a powerful shift in perspective. It allows us to step away from the trap of expecting things to be a certain way and being annoyed that they are not. Instead, Curiosity makes us intrigued as to what new pieces of information may appear in a portion of the world that is unfamiliar to us, that is filled with innovative perspectives and unexpected opportunities. It's something that Professor Adam Grant, from the University of Pennsylvania, says some experts may need to embrace more. He argues that the more familiar we become with our field, the less we might see new and unexpected things. He considers that two of the most important skills we can have are those cornerstones of Curiosity, the ability to rethink and unlearn.

BENEFITS OF CURIOSITY

Curiosity encourages us to be drawn to the intrigue and pleasure of experiencing something new, so it is linked to innovation and creativity. We can observe this in the house of inventor Edwin Land. In the 1940s, his Curious young daughter asked him why photos took days to develop. Inspired, he headed for the lab and designed the instant film 'Polaroid' camera. When we are Curious we are also more present, as we pay more attention to our senses to observe what is happening rather than what we expected. It helps us feel more alive, improves relationships, and gives us those moments of insight that contribute to a richer and more satisfying life. This may be why it has been linked to many health benefits, including predicting longevity in older adults and being protective against cognitive and physical decline with age[21,22].

CURIOSITY AND CHANGE
Curiosity is a vital ingredient for managing change, as it helps us stay open to how things could be different from how they currently are and embrace the unpredictability of whatever newness shows up. But it's something we may have had less connection to in recent years. As children, we are Curious, asking, as we attempt to understand our world, 'Why is the sky blue? The grass green? Grown-ups cross? Etc.'. But adults can tire of such questions, and as we grow up, we may be taught to 'stop asking questions all the time'. In the next few chapters, we will be considering things that you may have thought were unchangeable and reliable truths and asking you to re-evaluate if they are as unchangeable and reliable as you thought. Curiosity will be an invaluable ally in making that process intriguing and insightful, so let's use that powerful Gateway State as we take an IW-focused look at how we see the world.

THE CLASH OF YOUR INNER AND OUTER WORLDS
Some philosophers have suggested we inhabit two worlds. The first is our inner world, which is how we think things should be and our expectations and dreams. The second is the external world of how other people think about and respond to those hopes, dreams, and plans. One way of thinking about the trouble, stuckness, and challenges we have in life is that they occur when our inner world comes into hard contact with the external world of other people's, sometimes less than positive, responses. As I'm sure you've noticed, other people don't always seem to share, support, or value those dreams that are most important to us.

This rather unsurprising fact does, however, seem to surprise us each time. And, worse still, we seem to have very few skills to deal with this mismatch between what we hoped for and what actually happens. Noticing this tendency to be surprised in this way leads us to the next topic, that of maps.

MAPS

We're all familiar with the idea of geographical maps that help us navigate from one place to another. For this section, I'd like you to consider a different type of map. Instead of one that represents everything we need to know about a geographical region, I'd like you to imagine one that represents everything you know about how your life, the world, people, in fact, everything 'works'. Let's call this your 'personal map of reality' or for short **MAPP** - with the extra **P** reminding us that it's our *personal* version of how things are, our own specific take on how the world is, and that probably differs in many ways from everyone else's MAPP.

Just as a detailed map of New York guides tourists effectively around New York, your MAPP is your guide to life. It helps us estimate how things will work, who we are, our skills and talents, and what we can and can't achieve. It predicts what things, situations, and people will be like and guides us on how to experience and respond to anything we come across.

So, our MAPP is our go-to reference point for understanding, predicting, and evaluating everything, so we can make wise decisions. But unlike a brilliantly reliable database of up-to-date, well-researched information, it's much more like the internet. And the internet, as we all know, is both a great source of reliable knowledge and, in equal parts, unfounded opinion. Some of the details of our MAPP are also filled in from quite questionable source materials. This includes information based on, for example:

- Generalisations created from a small number of experiences (which may not have been great examples of how the world works: My dad, brother and physics teacher were all tall. They all shouted a lot ->Tall people shout a lot).

- Advice from deeply wise teens who were 2 years older than us.
- Lessons in how to deal with emotions from tired, frustrated, and angry parents.
- Life tips from social media.
- Understanding relationships based on our hormonally charged, broken-hearted teenage experiences, etc.

And, of course, all of these important guiding events that informed the building of our MAPP were understood, processed, and interpreted by the much younger, and probably emotionally confused, us.

The philosopher, Alfred Korzybski identified this issue and described it using the phrase 'the map is not the territory' [23]. He pointed out that a map we use to navigate our way through a new city is a useful scaled-down version (map) of what we'll find on the ground (territory). But we recognise that the map is not exactly the same as the city itself, there are many differences between the two. For example, the roads are wider than they are on the map, and if the city has changed since the map was made and buildings have been demolished or replaced, there will be some areas where inaccuracies have crept in. When we get to the city, we may find that some of the details we see - that small, recently groomed dog being taken for a walk by the lady in a red coat and no shoes, the sports car crashing into a lamppost, etc. are not present on the map. The same is true even of modern internet-based maps, like Google Maps, which, although more accurate than paper maps, still can't tell us what we can see, smell, and hear on the street at this singular moment in time.

Of course, we know this and understand that the map is not a precise replica of what is happening on the street right now. But it's good enough to get us around the city, so we use it. After a while, we forget its approximate nature and trust it as a faithful guide to the place. When we return some years later, we get out our trusty map to guide us. But new buildings and roads have been built, without our knowledge. We find ourselves surprised when we can no longer get down that now-closed road, or when our plans to meet friends at 10 a.m. are destroyed because the train station we relied on to get into the centre of the city is now an art gallery. We've forgotten that maps are by nature approximate, imperfect, and inaccurate. This issue becomes even more pressing when we consider the MAPP we hold inside our heads. It's so useful as a general and approximate guide to what might happen. But, like all maps, it is also approximate, imperfect, and inaccurate. Like the city street map that served us so well in the past, over time we forget that it was only ever intended as a rough guide to deal with the world at that point in time. Instead, we've started to treat it as if it's the true and correct version of how the world really is. This means we are guiding ourselves through the world, making some of our decisions based on partial remembrances of past events; imagining our past experiences will be a useful way to predict the future; and approaching adult situations with a child's version of who we are, what we (as a child) can and can't do. It's amazing, based on this, that we make as many good decisions as we do. This is because these MAPPs are editable, so we can, and do, update them. I've found in my work that some aspects of clients' MAPPs often need a bit of re-exploring for them to get the change they want. In these next chapters, we're going to be looking at some of the common areas where inaccurate pieces of information have been mistaken for truth. And to develop IW, the wisest thing to do is clear up these areas. Let's start this process with the next IWT.

IWT 5: Being Curious about the MAPP

This IWT will reconnect us with the Gateway State of Curiosity. Doing that will allow us to stay open as we explore our MAPPs. It will remind us that MAPPS are approximate, often inaccurate, and may need updating from time to time. Working from an outdated MAPP is the cause of many problems, so this is an essential step along the journey of developing IW. Get prepared as before. Make sure there is about 1 metre of space in front of you. Stand in the 'You' position and take 5 deep, easy breaths.

1. Start by reconnecting with a memory of being Curious, in the same way, we connected with 'Trust' in IWT 1. Allow your mind to drift back through the thousands of memories that you've collected throughout your life, to a time when you had a deep sense of Curiosity. These common examples that follow may help you choose one. Consider a time when:
    a. You had time on your hands to explore a new place, for example, an intriguing old city, or a naturally beautiful landscape. You wandered around, interested to see what would show up. You had no particular agenda or expectation; you were just interested in what you could find.
    b. You visited a museum, art gallery, or cinema. You weren't sure what was on, but you were interested in finding out. You wandered around intrigued, choosing which things to look at and wondering what was going to happen next on this unstructured trip.
    c. A friend highly recommended you read a book, watch a film, listen to a song, or visit a restaurant, but gave you no details of what it was about, only that you'd find it interesting. So, you did, approaching it with a sense of Curiousness as to what you'd experience and why they hadn't told you more.
    d. You met up with someone you'd not seen for a long time and were Curious about how much they'd changed, what they'd been doing since you last met.
    e. You were excited when someone who knows you well unexpectedly gave you a surprise gift-wrapped present.

f. You took a course/activity, but as it was new to you, you weren't completely sure what it involved, but you were Curious to find out.

g. You were on the internet searching for something - and a link to something else interesting caught your attention. You clicked and followed it, and another link and another... you lost track of time and discovered all sorts of unexpected new pieces of fascinating information.

h. You might want to step into the shoes of somebody you think of as being incredibly Curious. This may be someone you know personally or someone from history (such as Da Vinci, Galileo, Newton, Einstein, Picasso, Dali, etc.).

2. As you step fully into whichever one you choose, notice what you can:

a. **See** around you.

b. **Hear** what's going on around you as well as what's going on inside your head.

c. **Feel** physically (your breathing and posture, the temperature on your skin) and emotionally.

3. If that feeling and sensation were to have a colour, what colour would it be? Let that colour flow throughout your body, becoming even stronger and deeper with each breath.

4. As before, from where you are now - the 'You' position (noted by the dotted-line circle with the arrow pointing to the RIGHT in the diagram), step into the space just in front of you (the solid-line circle)- marked 'Inner Coach'. Then turn around 180 degrees so you are looking back towards the space you were just standing in (as shown by the arrow pointing to the LEFT). In this solid-line circle, you will be taking the role of the Inner Coach. See the 'You' still standing in that dotted-line circle right in front of you - in the 'You' position.

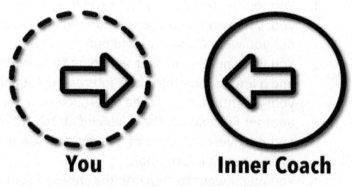

You   **Inner Coach**

5. Ask the 'You' over there, out loud, 'When did you see someone who, without knowing it, made a very poor decision that was based on outdated or incorrect information from their MAPP?'
6. Step back into the 'You' in the dotted-line circle and answer, out loud again, your Inner Coach's question.
7. Step back to the Inner Coach, and ask, 'What does that teach you about the power of MAPPs?'
8. Step back into the 'You' and answer.

We'll be exploring the power of MAPPs, the beliefs we buy into as a result of them, and how to change and update them in the next few chapters. Our first stop on that journey is to look at our MAPPs of health.

'Common sense is not so common.' - Voltaire

CHAPTER 11: CURIOSITY - MAPPS OF YOUR BRAIN AND BODY.

From our earlier exploration of the nervous system, you may recall how it manages both how the body is working - controlling the muscles, body temperature, digestion, hormone production, etc. - *and* all our thinking and emotions. This realisation makes it easier to understand how:

- Our thoughts and emotions can affect our body - an example of this is how being embarrassed (an emotional response to thinking) results in blushing (a physical response of diverting more blood into the capillaries in the face).
- And how what's going on in our body can affect how we are feeling and thinking - for example, the well-documented effects that exercise has on improving our mood[24].

When I first learnt about this mind-brain-body relationship, it ran counter to everything I'd been told about the body and the mind. In my education, they were treated as very different, unconnected things. Much of this was because the body has a physical existence - you can touch, see, weigh, and measure it - but the mind doesn't exist in that same physical way. Because of these huge differences - one being physical and the other not, academics, and especially the 17th-century French philosopher and scientist, René Descartes, reasoned they must be unconnected and unable to affect each other.

The fact that we understand much about the body but know so little about the mind, only makes matters more complicated. There's little agreement on 'what' the mind is or 'where' it's located. The ancient Greeks suspected it was in the stomach because that's where emotions often showed up. We can still hear this in idioms like 'swallowing down anger', 'they made me feel sick to my stomach', and 'I felt punched in the gut by their criticism'. Current thinking includes ideas that it's either in the brain or in our three brains. Yes, we have three brains! These are large collections of nervous tissue which seem to act partially independently from each other. 1) The brain in your head 2) the cardiac

76

nerve plexus around your heart and 3) the solar nerve plexus around your stomach. Some instead think it's present throughout the body rather than in one location, and others think that it's also outside of us as well. Stay Curious here, as research lends some support to this last idea. The electromagnetic field produced by the electrical signals running in our nervous system has been measured, and it extends beyond our body. As a result, being near others involves an interaction between your field and theirs[25]. But whichever of these is correct, it shows just how much missing information there is in our MAPPs about the mind, so it's no wonder we're unsure of how it might interact with the body.

Over the last 50 years this disconnect between the mind-brain-body often called the 'mind-body problem' has been challenged by the work of many researchers. They've identified just how much these systems interact and the wealth of data and published papers clearly show that the old model of the mind-brain-body being separate needs to be retired. To cover all that research here would fill several books but I think two brief pieces highlight this interactivity well.

First, when researchers studied experienced meditators (a thinking activity) they found changes in two body systems (a physical effect). Compared to non-mediators, they had a better-developed part of the brain (the insula) and an improvement in immune system function and an increased ability to fight off infections[17].

Second, another set of studies found that helping your gut health by drinking probiotic yoghurt (a physical intervention) also resulted in a reduction in depressive symptoms (an emotional effect)[26]. This is probably because, in the main nerve that connects the gut to the brain, the vagus nerve, most of the signals travel upward from the gut to the brain, so changes happening down below affect the brain above.

Hopefully, the above brief exploration of the 'mind-body problem' and how thoughts, feelings and physical health are interrelated develops and updates your MAPP of how the body, brain and mind are interconnected. One of the benefits of this more accurate MAPP is that it opens up new routes to help you affect your health. As the brain manages the body, then by using your brain differently it is possible to have a positive influence on your health. If that sounds new to you, then this is a great chance to be Curious. It may take you more exploration to update your MAPP on how you can affect your health in this way. You may find some of the research on how using this mind-brain-body connection can directly affect your physical health useful to support this change in perspective [2,27] . You can also read any of my other books on the subject or discover it for yourself by learning the Lightning Process (lightningprocess.com). Direct practical experience of this connection is a great way to change your MAPP, it certainly was for me when I started my recovery journey into this new updated version of the world. The next IWT gives you a simple way to explore for yourself practical ways to use this information.

IWT 6: The Benefits Of Calm

The state of being calm is such a common one that people don't access enough and is often needed for change. When you're angry, frustrated, annoyed, stressed, overwhelmed, etc., being able to find your way to feeling calm would be a valuable skill to have. It is also a great way to boost your health. This is because stress, especially when present for the long term, is quite damaging to the body and mind. It:

- Increases blood pressure and raises your pulse.
- Negatively affects your blood sugar levels.
- Disrupts your immune system function.
- Prevents sleep and clear thinking.
- Interrupts good digestion.
- And releases numerous powerful chemicals and hormones into the body.

Finding ways to feel calm is therefore not only good for your mental health, it's great for your physical health too, as it reverses the effects of stress and promotes the more nurturing functions in the body such as growth, repair, and recovery.

If you have a smartwatch that can measure your heart rate (or a device for checking your blood pressure) you can discover just how quickly you can influence your health with this technique by taking readings before and after. If you don't have access to those devices, it's fine. The technique will, of course, still work. Instead, you can measure the change by how you feel afterwards and by noting more long-term changes, such as how much your well-being, sleeping patterns, levels of calm, etc. improve from using all these tools.

DAILY PRACTICE

As developing calmness is such an important skill to build IW, I'd recommend you practice this technique, IWT 6, daily. You might want to record these steps on your phone, with pauses in between each step, and play them back as a guide to help you through the process. If you do, make sure your voice is really slow, calm and relaxing as you make the recording.

Get prepared as before. If you can, measure your heart rate or blood pressure first. This time, find a comfortable place to sit and take 5 deep, easy breaths.

1. Allow your mind to drift back through the thousands of memories that you've collected throughout your life, to a time when you had a deep sense of being calm and relaxed. Many types of moments may stand out for you. The common examples that follow may help you choose one.
    a. You may recall a time on holiday in a particular place, and, by just recalling it, you find yourself transported straight back there.
    b. It may be that feeling at the end of a busy day, when you've finished that project, moved house, stayed up late with friends, got home from travelling, and hit the bed feeling that special tired feeling that comes from a great but full day and being back in your own space. Connect with

snuggling down in your bed, feeling at peace with
the world.

    c. It may be that you take yourself into the future to
the most relaxing place that you could ever
imagine. Somewhere that has been completely
designed for you and your relaxation requirements.
Everything about it makes you feel relaxed, from
the temperature of the air around you to the
beautiful views, the deeply calming environment,
the gentle sounds, and the stillness.

    d. You might want to step into the shoes of somebody
you think of as being incredibly calm. It may be
someone you know personally or someone you've
heard about (such as the Buddha, etc.), it can even
be a cat or dog peacefully dozing in the warm
sunshine.

2. Whichever one you choose, allow yourself to fully connect
with and immerse yourself in that experience. As you step
fully into it, notice what you can:

    a. **See** around you.

    b. **Hear** what's going on around you as well as what's
going on inside your head.

    c. **Feel** physically (your breathing and posture, the
temperature on your skin) and emotionally.

3. If that feeling and sensation were to have a colour, what
colour would it be? Let that colour flow throughout your
body, becoming even more profound with each breath.

4. Spend at least three minutes connecting with this calm. If
at any point you find your mind drifting, and in the early
stages there is a good chance it will, just gently bring
yourself back to your chosen memory of calmness. This is
all part of the neuroplastic process of retraining your brain
to make calmness your starting point.

5. Finish the IWT by connecting to what it feels like to have
this calmness show up, through practice, in all the places,
spaces, relationships, conversations, and communications

and projects you move through. Noticing how it softens everything, bringing you to these situations in a different way and helping to reset your resting levels of calmness to a new even healthier level.

At the end of this IWT recheck your heart rate/blood pressure, it should have lowered to a much calmer resting level (resting heart rates are usually 60-70 beats per minute but can be lower). I've just done the exercise and my resting heart rate which is 57 reduced to 45. Blood pressure does depend on age, and advice has varied over time as to the ideal levels. Current advice is that someone in their 20s would expect to be 110/80 and in their 50s 120/80, from the SPRINT study in 2017 [28]. Usually, people notice a 5-to-20-point decrease in both readings after this IWT, and the more you do it the more this becomes your baseline heart rate and blood pressure.

TAKEAWAYS

In this chapter, you've begun to explore your MAPPs of health and how the body and mind can interact. Hopefully, in this process, your MAPP has become more complete, accurate, and enriched. You've also discovered how you can access one of the most commonly missing states, that of calm. By doing that, you can see and experience physiological changes in your body, whether it's feeling how your breathing is easier, you're sleeping better or, if you've measured it, how your heart rate or blood pressure has changed. Each time you access calm, you will be boosting your health, so think of this as giving your body a little gift every time you do it.

This theme of change and exploring our MAPPS to see if they need updating is the focus of the next few chapters.

'Each Time You Access Calm, You Will Be Boosting Your Health.'

CHAPTER 12: CURIOSITY - MAPPS OF CHANGE

Our next stop on our journey into Curiosity is to explore how change works and the power of beliefs. Change is a major theme throughout this book, so it's important to understand what makes change possible and what happens when we have problems with it. Beliefs are very linked to how easily we can make changes and achieve our goals. You may have noticed these popping up throughout the book so far, for example, in the last chapter, we looked at our beliefs about the mind-brain-body link and how much we can influence our health. Beliefs are the things that keep our MAPPS intact. Much like a tent is held up by the tent poles and guy-ropes, or a hammock relies on the trees it's slung from to stay intact, beliefs maintain our MAPPs structure. As a result, we need to look very carefully at our beliefs, as although our lives move on, they often stay the same and may need some updating.

CHANGE IS...

Let's begin with our next MAPP update by considering what we think about 'change'. Take a few moments to consider your thoughts and beliefs about change. There are many different ones, some that are commonly held by society in general and others less so - but what do you think? Consider these common questions about change and notice what answers your MAPP gives you.

- Is it easy to do?
- Is change a slow or fast process?
- Does it take quite some time to change something?
- Are some things easier than others to change?
- Do some people find change easier than others?
- Does it make a difference if you've had an issue for a long time?
- Or how old you are?

Once you've considered your answers and thoughts about change read on.

IS CHANGE HARD?

Here are three important and conflicting MAPPS of change.

1. Change is considered to be constantly occurring in the universe, with everything changing from complex to more simple structures. Physicists call this universal move towards change and simplicity the concept of entropy. A sandwich left on a windowsill is an example of this. It will not stay the same forever. It might be pecked at by birds or slowly rot and disintegrate. Over time, the complex structures and molecules in the sandwich become broken down into simpler ones. So, change is an inevitable process that affects everything. And yet...
2. How many people seem to be stuck with the same problems year after year; the same New Year's resolutions; the same hopes and dreams that they never fulfil; the same problems, habits, addictions, etc.? Contrary to point 1, this suggests that change is difficult and avoidable. And yet...
3. How many things have you changed in your life? How many different hairstyles have you had? How has the style of your clothes changed since you were 5, 10, a teenager, and onwards? Do you buy new books or just reread the same ones? We all know people who have managed to make huge changes in their lives, to leave difficult relationships, move countries, find new careers, give up smoking, alcohol, or drugs, or take up exercise or a new hobby.

So, change is an interesting phenomenon. Some people believe (have a MAPP), from personal experience, that change is difficult. But the truth is more nuanced:

- Some change, for some people, sometimes, seems very hard.
- And for others, the same change seems easy.

Some people manage to change long-established patterns that others find challenging to change such as habits, addictions, or leaving toxic relationships. This suggests that it is possible to change even long-standing behaviours, beliefs, or issues, that others find difficult to shift.

Whenever we discover someone who has easily changed a habit that we've been struggling to shift, we might at first be annoyed, but if we can remain Curious, it can be an opportunity to discover something new. If we could work out, in enough detail, exactly HOW they have made that change, we might be able to discover and take on whatever steps worked for them. That process is called 'modelling' (described in the early works on NLP[29]) and it is a valuable skill for helping people make change. This book contains the results of some of my in-depth modelling research into how people make a range of important changes in their lives; how they become kinder, coach themselves, get to be curious and tap into their wisdom, etc. You've already experienced some of the value of this research in the IWTs covered so far, and because they are based on modelling others' successes, it provides a rapid way to make change, shift your MAPP and take on new behaviours.

IS CHANGE SLOW?

The next MAPP issue we often need to address concerns the speed of change. Some think that if a behaviour has been in place for a long time, or the issue is a big one, then it will take a long time to change. But this isn't completely true either. There are many examples of people changing decades-old issues rapidly.

This video of Paul resolving his strong and long-term phobic response to the sound of nails being drawn down a chalkboard is a good example.

Click on the link, https://youtu.be/_tKRl6ZH8w0 or use your

smartphone's camera to scan the QR code and watch the video.

Paul had this issue for three decades and resolved it in about 15 minutes. Did that surprise you? If so, it suggests you have a MAPP about change that may need an update.

So, how do some people make change so quickly? It might be the result of the timing being right, new tools being available, or new perspectives showing up in their lives, but, as in the example of Paul, people do shift old patterns, and they can often do it quickly.

Just looking at these two common but outdated MAPPs, 'change is hard' and 'change is slow' identifies how much we might be holding onto unhelpful beliefs and expectations about change. But these are not the only ones, below is a list of others that commonly show up for people. Although they are not that accurate or helpful, due to the amount of time we have heard them, they can start to become very convincing.

Some MAPPs for Lack of Change:

- You can't teach an old dog new tricks.
- If something has been there for a long time, it will take an equal amount of time to change.
- Changes take a long, long time - it takes thousands of repetitions before it becomes stable.
- Quick change is superficial, it never lasts.
- This just can't be changed. It's just the way I am.
- Damaging habits are more difficult to break than good ones.
- This kind of thing is different - it's more difficult to change.
- Other people are different from me, so although they can change this, I don't think I can.

Most of us have had times in our lives when we've felt some of these ways about change. Which ones have you found yourself saying from time to time, or have a library of evidence for being true?

IWT 7: The Belief Exercise

Take a piece of paper. Make two columns, one headed 'Changed', the other 'Not changed yet'.

1. In the 'Changed' column write down 5 big things you've managed to change in your life. It might include habits, friendships, jobs, how you feel about yourself, etc.
2. In 'Not changed yet' write down those things you've not managed to shift yet.
3. Then consider the beliefs you have about change when looking at the 'Changed' column.
4. Pause and consider the beliefs you have about change when looking at the 'Not changed yet' column. How many of them fit with the 'Some MAPPS for Lack of Change' list, or have you discovered some additional one to add to that list?
5. Which of those beliefs would you like to change today?

You're going to take these beliefs and change the ones you no longer want, using IWT 7 Compass Process. But before you do that, we need to cover the nature of beliefs and how to spot them.

THE PROBLEM WITH BELIEFS

You may have already identified that these MAPPs, and the beliefs that come with them, can be incredibly helpful or cause huge problems. They can help us, by making us believe supportive things about our abilities or futures. They can also unintentionally prevent us from experiencing anything new, dismissing any information that doesn't fit with our MAPP, which may be in need of an update. Let's imagine somebody with the limiting belief of 'low self-worth', who feels that they are just not very good at anything and unworthy of praise.

- When something they do goes well and they get acknowledged for it, they will likely discount this information. They may reject it thinking, 'Well I was lucky that time' or 'That person was just giving me praise to be

nice, they don't really mean what they're saying', and so on.
- But when they do something that goes badly, or they receive criticism, the door is wide open for that information to come in and join the party, as it fits with their MAPP and beliefs.

The trickiest thing about beliefs is even spotting that they are beliefs. This is because, as we trust the accuracy of our MAPP more than new information, these beliefs show up as 'truths'. So how can we become more aware of our limiting beliefs? Taking stock to review how you're thinking about things is a great starting point, as you discovered in the previous 'Belief Exercise'. The next section provides some further tools that will help make this process of spotting beliefs easier.

Language And Belief Detection
Listening out for certain words will show up the presence of beliefs. Key ones to watch out for are statements including the words:

- Always.
- All.
- Never.
- Every time.
- Everybody.

Or generalisations, where a whole group of people, things or events are described as all having the same characteristics:

- All women are...
- All men can't...
- Every party is...
- Snakes are never...

Sometimes the 'all' isn't even used, as in, 'Men are so untidy', 'Snakes are nasty'.

As soon as you hear these words you want to pause and consider if it is:

1. Factual and **completely** accurate, in **all** cases - if the answer is NO it's a belief.

2. Or a guess, an **opinion,** or **mostly/sometimes** accurate - if the answer is YES it's a belief.

Watch out for 'it's **mostly** true' type statements such as, 'It's mostly true that **everything I do fails'**. The danger of this type of statement is that it makes us feel like '**we fail all the time'**. However, closer inspection shows that its true meaning is 'I don't fail **all the time,** because **I get it right sometimes'**.

Having identified the presence of the belief by using those two rules, we next need to assess the belief statement.

IWT 8: The Simple, Big Question

Often, we assess beliefs by judging if 'it is **correct or incorrect**?' There is a problem with this though. Due to the bias that we already identified in trusting the accuracy of beliefs we already hold, we're going to need another way to assess them. A better way to do this is by asking one simple and incredibly important question:

'Is this belief **useful** to me?'

Take the example of 'I will never be able to pass my driving test'.

If we've taken it 4 times without passing and we use the rule 'is it correct?' we might be tempted to see this as 'yes it's **true**, I'll never pass'. Unfortunately, if you continue to have that belief, then it's going to make developing your driving skills and passing much more difficult. This is because if (our MAPP says) 'it's impossible to achieve', then why even bother?

If we ask instead, 'Is it **useful** to me?', the answer is much clearer and more helpful. We can see that buying into this belief is not going to help you pass, and stepping away from this MAPP of the world will be more useful.

As our beliefs can be quite convincing and may stop us from re-evaluating that MAPP there's an IWT specifically designed to help us use this question. It adds some new skills to the IWTs you've already learned.

First, choose something that you suspect is a limiting belief.

Get prepared as before. This time, find a chair or bed that is safe to comfortably stand on (if that's not possible see the notes at the end for alternative steps). Arrange it so the 'You' and 'Inner Coach' are in the usual places and the chair/bed is behind the Inner Coach position (see the grey square in the diagram). Stand in the 'You' position, making sure there are about 2 metres of space in front of you, and take 5 deep, easy breaths.

1. In the 'You' position (shown by the dotted-line circle with the arrow pointing to the RIGHT in the diagram). Reconnect with the Gateway State of 'Curiosity'.
2. As before, using this diagram as a guide, step into the space just in front of you (the solid-line circle) marked 'Inner Coach'.
3. Then turn around 180 degrees so you are looking back towards the space you were just standing in (as shown by the arrow pointing to the LEFT).

You   **Inner Coach**

4. In this solid-line circle, you will be taking the role of the Inner Coach. See the 'You' still standing in that dotted-line circle right in front of you - in the 'You' position. Looking directly at the 'You' over there, say out loud, as you did the Self-Kindness IWT 4:

    a. 'I'm so proud of you and all that you have achieved.'

    b. List a few things that you know took a lot of effort from you to make happen: 'Like that time when you...'

    c. 'I see these qualities in you...'

    d. 'You're really good at...' (List a few stand-out examples of skills and abilities that you know you have. No one else is listening, so it's ok to say them out loud. Examples include being patient with kids/making fabulous soup/gardening/making friends, etc. but choose YOUR own).

    e. 'And I really like that about you.'

    f. 'I know you've had to deal with some stuff in your life and you always keep going.'

    g. 'I know, like everyone else, although you don't always get it right all the time, you always do your very best.'

    h. 'I think you are a truly amazing person.'

    i. 'You (add your name), are enough'.

    j. 'I love you.'

5. Step back into the 'You' in the dotted-line circle and feel how it feels to hear your Inner Coach say these things to you. Let this in, then take some time to enjoy those feelings of Self-Kindness and acknowledgement. Doing these steps first will make it much easier to answer the Simple, Big Question coming up. Now turn your attention to the belief you want to assess.

6. Step back to the Inner Coach and say to 'You':

    a. I know this has been something that, because of past experiences, has shaped your world for some time.

    b. But it may be outdated.

7. Now climb up onto the chair/bed behind the Inner Coach. You'll find that physically stepping up and back increases that sense of distance and perspective even more. From

here you will see the belief differently with much less emotion and more rationality. Ask the 'You' over there the Simple, Big Question **'Is this way of thinking useful for you?'** Another way of phrasing this is to ask, **'Is this your wisest choice?'** Return to the 'You' position and notice your answer - it should be 'NO'*.

8. Step back to the chair/bed and ask, 'Is there anything useful that you need to learn from this, that helps your future, before you can let it go completely?'

9. Step back into 'You' and notice your answer. You might be surprised at what comes up from your IW. Take a few deep breaths as you allow yourself to absorb these important learnings into your body, gut, heart, and mind.

10. Finally, reconnect with the Gateway State of Kindness again and feel it flowing through you and anyone else involved. Flowing through those old past events, softening, shrinking, blurring out, and giving you a new, healthier perspective on those outdated beliefs. Freeing yourself to step into your life in a new way. Feel how this future feels as you explore it with this sense of ease and flow. Notice how you feel different now.

Notes:

- If you aren't able to easily or safely access a suitable chair or bed, then you can imagine yourself being one floor above where you are and looking down.
- Some people find it easier to do the process in an upstairs room and imagine seeing the 'You' down there, outside at ground level.
- *As you practise this IWT you may start to apply it to more complex issues. Sometimes in steps 6/7, you may find some sense of resistance, objection, or reluctance to let it go. This is fine, as there will be excellent reasons for this that need to be listened to. Another process, IWT 17, working with Parts, may resolve this for you, but in cases

of trauma or serious adverse events in your past, you may need the help of an experienced practitioner. Remember, IW doesn't mean doing it on your own, part of wisdom is knowing when to seek extra support, and this is something that will be part of the fascinating topics we'll explore in the next chapters.

- You may notice in step 9 you absorbed these changes into your three brains, the head, heart, and gut that we met in Chapter 11.

When you've done this a few times, you may find you can shortcut this process sometimes by just asking the Simple, Big Question. The realisation that this belief isn't useful is very powerful and now that we've identified that we have some beliefs that are not useful, it's time to change them even further.

THE FRAGILITY OF BELIEFS

It is worth considering some important aspects of beliefs that are often forgotten.

1. All the beliefs you have now were taught to you at some point. You weren't born with them. That's why, because of the different experiences they've had, different people have different beliefs. It's also why different cultures believe that, for example, having a tan, wearing a bikini, or eating certain foods is good, immoral, normal, or weird.
2. As beliefs are things we have learnt, we need to identify the source and reliability of this teaching. The teachers at everyone's 'school of beliefs' were usually:
   a. Experts and authority figures
      What makes someone an authority figure? Well, they just need to be somebody that we trust, rely on, and think has deeper experience and insight than we do. The source of this wisdom, therefore, can often be quite dubious - it may have been your bigger 7-year-old sister when you were five.

b. Repeated experience.
This can be just as problematic. As we now know, beliefs only allow in information that supports them and discount anything that doesn't fit with them. This means our experience is a biased version of the world. We give much more value to the experiences that fit that belief - this is what is behind the 'It's mostly true that **everything I do fails**' statements. This makes experience a sometimes useful and sometimes unreliable guide to the future. As we built these MAPPs and formed these beliefs when we were much younger and less aware of the nuances of the world, basing today's decisions on judgements we made at 5, 7, 10 or 15 may not always be best.

3. The authority figure that was the source of the belief is probably not present in the same way in our lives now. So, if we still have those beliefs, it is **we** who are continuing to keep these beliefs alive.

There are powerful and positive consequences of understanding the above issues with beliefs. It helps us recognise that maybe we don't need to continue to be trapped by those old beliefs. Earlier, we recognised that we have changed our beliefs throughout our lives. When we combine these factors, it frees us up to recognise that it's important we review our beliefs and, if it's valuable to do so, are perfectly positioned to change them forever.

RECIPE FOR UPDATING A BELIEF

Based on the above exploration of beliefs, there are four key elements required to update and change a belief. We need to:

1. Stop having our experience predict what will happen in the future, as sometimes those past experiences were unreliable.

2. Recognise that sometimes experts (like our 7-year-old big sister) don't have all the information and may inaccurately state things as truths.
3. Reconnect with times when we powerfully and radically changed our future and remind ourselves that huge change happens.
4. Recall how it feels to decide to show the world that you can achieve more than anyone expected.

This next IWT uses these important pieces of information about how beliefs are formed and updated to help you disentangle yourself from the ones you don't want anymore and to let them go...and introduces us to our next Gateway State, Shift.

'Our MAPP, Like All Maps, Is Approximate, Imperfect, And Inaccurate.'

CHAPTER 13: SHIFT - LETTING BELIEFS GO

Shift

The Gateway State of 'Shift' is simple to understand and incredibly powerful to use. It describes that moment when suddenly everything changes. Where you have a sense of a door opening to a whole new future or that a switch has been flicked on. Suddenly, the world feels radically different, and everything that was stuck is now in flow. It's that vibrant experience of everything being possible. When we experience life from the Gateway State of Shift, it reminds us of how much infinite possibility there is in the world, how we are powerful agents of change and what we do does make a difference. Just by connecting with this state, we become awake to the possibility of something completely different showing up. There are so many examples in everybody's life of this. It might be the extraordinariness of having a baby, embarking on a brand-new career, moving out of an old, stifling relationship, starting a new adventure, uncovering a spiritual realm to your life, recovering from a serious illness, or coming across some wisdom in a book, film, song, or conversation that makes you feel completely different about your life. One powerful moment from life always reminds me of this Gateway State of Shift. It was six months after my hand injury. I hoped and trusted that I'd recover, but, checking every day, there was still no sign of it. It's a strange feeling when your fingers don't work. You decide to move your fingers, and a message is sent along your nerves to instruct them to move. But because the connection between the fingers and the brain is cut, the signal never gets to the muscles that move the fingers. So, the fingers just sit there like lifeless sausages, completely unresponsive. But on this particular day, as I sat in a lecture with some friends - and I can remember the room in great detail, the lighting, the temperature, and what I was wearing - I checked as usual and, for the first time since my injury, saw the very first tiny movement in my fingers. It wasn't a full movement, it was just a minute flicker, but everything changed in that moment. I now knew that the nerve, contrary to the experts' opinions, had regrown and the movement had started to return. Imagine how that felt. Whenever I reconnect with this memory, I'm once again reminded of how change is absolutely possible and that the future is full of opportunities waiting to unfold.

IWT 9: Shift

Set aside 5 minutes for this technique, which will reconnect you to some powerful moments of Shift in your past. Get prepared as before.

1. Allow your mind to drift back through the thousands of memories that you've collected throughout your life, to a time when you had this powerful sense of Shift. As described above, there are many types of moments that may stand out for you.
    a. Choose one that really calls to you from your personal experience.
    b. Or you may be inspired by hearing about someone else's journey and connect with how they experienced a shift in their lives. There are so many examples, including Copernicus, who realised, contrary to the strongly held views of the time, that the sun, not the earth, was the centre of the solar system; or the Buddha, who was born a wealthy prince but gave up all his worldly comforts to be an ascetic and seeker of enlightenment.
4. Whichever type of memory you choose, allow yourself to fully connect with and immerse yourself in that experience. As you step fully into it, notice what you can:
    a. **See** around you.
    b. **Hear** what's going on around you as well as what's going on inside your head.
    c. **Feel** physically (such as your breathing and posture, the temperature on your skin, etc.) and emotionally.
5. If that feeling and sensation were to have a colour, what colour would it be? Let that colour flow throughout your body, becoming even stronger and deeper with each breath.

6. Quite often, people feel a powerful urge to express this extraordinary moment with some kind of movement or sound. I've heard people say it's like a superman pose or a fanfare 'Dah-dahhh!!', a sense of firework exploding with a 'ka-pow!!' or a wide opened armed 'Yeahhh!!' If this sounds fun to you, see what kind of movement or sound fits with your Shift.

Again, notice how great it feels to get in touch with this Gateway State. I'd recommend revisiting this IWT daily. Doing this, switches on the pathways of these 'Shift' memories and releases a range of neurochemicals and hormones throughout your body. And, because of neuroplasticity, the more you practice this, the easier you'll find it to get in touch with these memories. As you connect with this 'Shift' ask yourself, 'Where in the next few days or weeks would it be useful to re-access this feeling?'

IWT 10: Compass Process

This transformational IWT combines the Gateway State of Shift with many elements of IW that we've discovered so far. You'll find you'll be able to rapidly change limiting beliefs using this process.

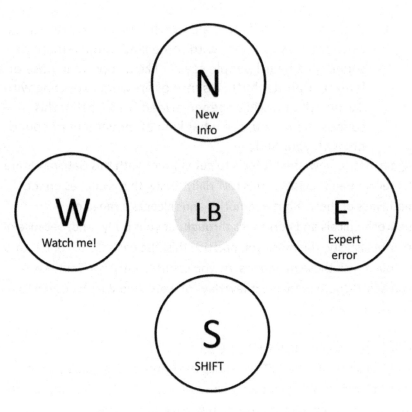

This looks a little different from the other IWT we've used so far, so let's begin with an overview of the key elements of this IWT using the diagram. The steps of the IWT itself will guide you through what to do in more detail.

The circle in the centre marked LB stands for the Limiting Belief. The other four circles, marked N, E, S, and W (after the compass points **N**orth, **E**ast, **S**outh, and **W**est), correspond to the four elements in the recipe for updating beliefs, from the previous chapter (listed below as a reminder).

1. Stop having our experience predict what will happen in the future.
2. Recognise that sometimes experts are wrong.
3. Reconnect with times when we powerfully and radically changed our future.

4. Recall how it feels to show the world that you can achieve more than anyone expected.

N is for **N**ew information.

Purpose: This addresses element 1, that we need to **stop having our experience predict** what will happen in **the future**, as sometimes those past experiences were unreliable.

State: Here you will reconnect with a time when you discovered your past experiences didn't predict the future well, and how being aware of this **N**ew information about how the world was, you changed your point of view.

E is for **E**xpert Error.

Purpose: This addresses element 2, that we need to recognise that **sometimes experts** (like our 7-year-old big sister) don't have all the information and state things as truths that **are incorrect**.

State: Here you will reconnect with a time when you discovered someone you used as a source of trusted information, an **E**xpert, got it wrong.

S is for **S**hift.

This addresses element 3, that we need to reconnect with times when **we powerfully and radically changed our future** and remind ourselves that huge change happens. Here you'll reconnect with the experience of radically changing things, the Gateway State of **S**hift.

W is for **W**atch me!

This addresses element 4, where we recall how it feels **to decide to show the world that we can** achieve more than anyone expected.

State: Here you will reconnect with what a persistent, free-spirited force of nature you are. You'll recall a time when you forged a path that went against what others predicted for your future and showed others that you were capable of more than they imagined.

The Steps

Get prepared in the usual way. This time, make sure you've got space for an imaginary circle that's 2 metres across. Although this IWT uses the compass points of N, E, S, and W, it's only to help you remember what to do in each position, you don't need to be facing the North Pole when at **North**.

Start by thinking about the belief that you want to change - you may want to choose one from the list you made in the beliefs exercise in Chapter 12. You may discover others as you go through the book and you can use this technique on each of them as needed.

1. Stand up and imagine holding this Limiting Belief in your hands. Notice, out of 10 how much you currently believe it. You will score it this way several times during the steps.
2. Imagine dropping it onto the floor in the centre of the space. As it hits the floor, see it flatten out. Allow your imagination to help you picture it - what colour, smell, texture, and size does it have? Ask yourself, 'Is it ok to change this?' If it is, then proceed, if not then read the section on 'Parts' Chapter 17 first.
3. Now spread it so it is really thin, maybe the thickness of a very thin pancake - if it were any thinner it would tear. Some people like to do this with their hands or feet. Notice how this starts to change how it feels, making it feel fragile and delicate. Notice how this reduces its score.
4. Stand in the **North** position. This is the place you will connect with gaining 'New Information'. To do this, recall a powerful experience of a time when you came across some new information that made you realise your previous understanding of something was in error. The new information may have been surprising, but you recognised it as a useful addition to your MAPP and you felt that sense of readjusting your worldview as a result. Examples can be positive or negative experiences,

examples include, getting a job that you were certain you wouldn't be offered; finding an event you were dreading to be surprisingly enjoyable; discovering someone you trusted didn't deserve your trust; seeing a politician you thought would lose, get elected. Once again, as you immerse yourself in that moment, deepen your experience of it by recalling what you can see, hear, and feel.

Now walk to the centre and pour this feeling of gaining 'New Information' into the Limiting Belief, noticing how it further weakens that belief. Rescore it again.

5. Move into the East position. This is the place you will connect with 'Expert Error'. Here you recall a powerful experience of a time when you realised the opinion of an expert or authority figure was wrong. They may have been very confident in their opinion, so you bought into it, but later you discovered they were in error. It could be a mechanic/builder who said this would fix your car/house at this cost and it turned out to not be so; a health care practitioner's limiting prognosis that turned out to not be correct, etc. Once again, as you immerse yourself in that moment, deepen your experience of it by recalling what you can see, hear and feel.

   Now walk to the centre and pour this feeling of 'Expert Error' into the weakened belief, noticing how it further undermines it. Rescore it again.

6. Move into the South position. This is the place you will connect with 'Shift' from the previous IWT. Here you recall a powerful experience of a time when something immense changed in your life. That sense of everything flipping, an inner revolution, that feeling of everything being in flow, where the things you took to be unchangeable just melted away and the future opened up. Once again, as you immerse yourself in that moment, deepen your experience of it by recalling what you can see, hear, and feel.

   Now walk to the centre and pour this feeling of 'Shift' into whatever remains of that belief, noticing how it further dissolves that belief. Rescore it again.

7. Move into the **W**est position. This is the place you will connect with 'Watch me!'. Here you recall a powerful experience of a time we connected with in IWT 1 when someone told you that a goal was impossible for you to attain, and your response was, 'That makes me even more determined to achieve it', or '*You* think I can't do it, **watch me** as I prove you wrong'. Once again, as you immerse yourself in that moment, deepen your experience of it by recalling what you can see, hear, and feel.

   Now walk to the centre and pour this feeling of '**W**atch me!' into any remaining dregs of that belief noticing how it further dissolves them. Rescore how you feel about it now. The chances are it will have lost all its power and faded away, as this happens in most cases. If it feels like it needs a little more work before it completely goes, then repeat steps 4-7 walking (or some people find it useful to dance) a few more times into the centre with the feelings at N, E, S, and W until the belief has lost all its power.

8. Now that the old Limiting Belief has gone, there's a space for a new Empowering Belief to take its place. State out loud the belief you'd love to have about this goal. Step into the centre and pour that vibrant, engaging new belief into that space. Feel it supporting you and flowing through you from the ground up to the sky. Feel how it feels to be in your future with this new belief as a part of every step of that journey. Take a few moments to notice how it enhances your:
    a. Relationships, communications, and the places you go.
    b. Your talents and abilities, actions, and behaviours.
    c. The way you spend your time and energy.
    d. Other beliefs you have about your future and who you really are.

e. Your ability to show up for others and make an even bigger difference to the things that are deeply important to you.

Having completed this technique, notice how different that feels. I'd recommend taking a break for a few minutes after this to let that important work process through your mind, brain, and body. Ideally, go for a walk in nature if you can. You might feel excited or a little tired as a result of the powerful work you have done, that will change how your future unfolds.

'SHIFT reminds us of how much infinite possibility there is in the world.'

CHAPTER 14: SHIFT - BLAME, RESPONSIBILITY, AND INFLUENCE

Our next use of the Gateway State of Shift is in sorting through some major issues and concepts that are essential to developing IW. Understanding blame, responsibility, and influence is so important to your health, happiness, and success that I've included a section about them in every book I've written.

There is often some confusion about what they mean, so let's start there. Dictionaries often define blame as thinking 'that someone or something did something wrong or is **responsible** for something bad happening'. While responsibility is 'having a duty to deal with, be accountable for, or to **blame** for something'. Here we can see how responsibility and blame are used interchangeably, but there are also some differences that need unpacking.

Blame is very much about finding fault and identifying who caused a particular problem. As a result, it focuses on the past. There are times when fault finding is useful. Discovering a problem's cause can help us solve it; 'Which part of this aeroplane was poorly designed and to blame for the accident?' But other examples; 'My past/dad/education is to blame for my actions', don't help us move forward to a better life. There are also some serious side effects of blaming, even if it's justified:

- It leaves us focused on the unchangeable past and on how things *should* have been.
- And suggests that, as the other person or thing caused the problem, *they*, and not us, need to fix it.

Unfortunately, as I'm sure you've already found out, this rarely works as a strategy for making things improve. That moment in time has now passed, that person may no longer be in our lives, or if they are, they may be unwilling to change - the only main benefit is that you get to be righteously annoyed with how much trouble ***they've*** caused.

Responsibility can also be used in the same way as blame. 'You're responsible for this mess, so clean it up', or 'You're responsible for us leaving the house late'. But there's an additional meaning that is useful to explore, where responsibility means to recognise what things are within our power to affect and what things are not. Here the meaning diverges from that of blame and becomes one of having the potential to *respond* differently and to exert **'influence'**.

We can see this in the case of the diabetic bus driver. Imagine being on a bus where the driver, who has diabetes, has not been managing his health or blood sugar levels well and collapses into a diabetic coma at the wheel. We can identify who's at fault for the fact that the bus is about to crash. It is clearly the bus driver. But of course, once he is unconscious, although he and his poor blood sugar management are to blame for the situation, he can't fix the issue. Identifying the cause here doesn't help much, as the bus driver's unmanaged blood sugar levels are in the past and unchangeable. Knowing the cause and who's to blame is not that relevant to finding a solution to this immediate crash problem.

It's more useful for the passengers to exert any influence they can on what happens next. Hopefully, they'll grab the steering wheel and save the day. The sense of influence is key here. In life, one of the things we have the most influence over is our power to choose how we perceive and respond to events. On the bus, there are several choices that create very different futures; we could find fault, get paralysed by fear, or take action. Our responses depend on how we are processing the events. Are we seeing them from a perspective of blame or influence?

Our guidebook to the world, our MAPP, may have a Blame focus. It may advise us that (a) the world *should* be a certain way and (b) we need to spend time finding who's at fault and the cause of this issue. This can result in perspectives and statements such as:

1. 'My boss was at fault for making me angry'.
2. 'My past was to blame for my actions'.
3. 'You're responsible for us leaving the house late'.

And although finding who's to blame seems like a reasonable thing to do, it may, as with the bus driver, be of little help. In these examples, the fault lies with:

1. The boss.
2. My past.
3. My partner.

But we're unlikely to get your boss or your past to change, and now that we're late, getting annoyed with your partner isn't going to make us on time or have a great evening out.

Instead, having a MAPP where our focus is on Influence can be more helpful. Considering each of these scenarios, can we:

1. Deal with our boss or our emotions differently?
2. Find ways to change how our past influences our current behaviours?
3. Find a way to stay relaxed and focus on the evening?

The answer to all of these is 'Yes!' We can see from this that, in many situations, although it is unfair that it falls to us because it is not our fault, the person who can most influence what happens next in your life is you. With practice, we can apply IW to find different responses to these, and many more events, that *shouldn't* be the way they are.

Stepping up and taking responsibility for having this influence may not always be the easiest or most comfortable thing to do. But it is the wisest choice. All the other options result in having others' behaviours direct how we feel (as in, 'the way he spoke made me angry') or wasting our energy blaming others and justifying why things aren't the way we want them to be.

Although it asks us to step up and deal with things differently, the decision to swap blame for influence is worth it. Making this shift will mean that you are actively making decisions about what you do with your time and energy. It also gives *you*, rather than your past, a chance to decide where your life goes. There will be a range of IWT we'll be covering that help you let go of blame and embrace your power to influence your future, including the one that follows.

IWT 11: Letting Go Of Blame And Taking Up Influence

You'll be familiar with some of the steps from IWT 8 'The Simple, Big Question'

First, choose something which you are still harbouring a grudge about. As usual, when you first use this IWT choose something mild. It could be something that happened in the near or distant past, some slight, negative comment or criticism, something that feels unjust, or where you feel someone has caused you problems. And when you think about it, it still stings in some way.

Spotting the word 'should' (you may have noticed I put it in italics in the earlier pages) may help this process. Examples are, 'They should/shouldn't have done that' and it can sometimes show up as 'They ought to', 'They mustn't' or 'They needed to'. Dr Albert Ellis, the founder of Rational Emotive Behavioural Therapy, often told his patients to 'stop should-ing all over yourself' (say it out loud to see why) as he recognised how damaging this pattern was for them.

It may well be true that someone else was to blame and should have acted differently, but they didn't, and unfortunately, you are the one who is still suffering as a result of holding onto the blame. Quite often, the other person has moved on and forgotten it, and you're the one still dwelling on it and feeling annoyed about it. There is a quote, often attributed to the Buddha, but it originates from Alcoholics Anonymous, who are pretty big on forgiveness, that says, 'Holding onto anger is like swallowing poison and expecting someone else to die'. So, if you're ready to stop sipping that harmful beverage, let's go. Get prepared as before. Find a chair or bed that is safe to comfortably stand on (if that's not possible see the notes at the end for alternative steps). Arrange the 'You' and 'Inner coach' as usual, with the chair/bed behind the Inner Coach position (see the grey square in the diagram). Stand in the 'You' position, making sure there is about 2 metres of space in front of you, and take 5 deep, easy breaths.

1. In the 'You' position (shown by the dotted-line circle with the arrow pointing to the RIGHT in the diagram). Reconnect with the Gateway State of 'Shift' you accessed in IWT 9 and the Compass Process

2. As before, using this diagram as a guide, step into the space just in front of you (the solid-line circle) marked 'Inner Coach'.

3. Then turn around 180 degrees so you are looking back towards the space you were just standing in (as shown by the arrow pointing to the LEFT).

You   Inner Coach

4. In this solid-line circle, you will be taking the role of the Inner Coach. See the 'You' still standing in that dotted-line circle right in front of you - in the 'You' position. Looking directly at the 'You' over there, say out loud, as you did the Self-Kindness IWT 4:
   a. 'I'm so proud of you and all that you have achieved.'
   b. 'Like that time when you...' (List a few things that you know took a lot of effort from you to make happen).
   c. 'I see these qualities in you...'
   d. 'You're really good at...' (List a few stand-out examples of skills and abilities that you know you have. No one else is listening, so it's ok to say them out loud. Examples include being patient with kids/making fabulous soup/gardening/making friends, etc. but choose YOUR own).

e. 'And I really like that about you.'
f. 'I know you've had to deal with some stuff in your life and you always keep going.'
g. 'I know, like everyone else, although you don't always get it right all the time, you always do your very best.'
h. 'I think you are a truly amazing person.'
i. 'You (add your name), are enough'.
j. 'I love you.'

5. Step back into the 'You' in the dotted-line circle and feel how it feels to hear your Inner Coach say these things to you. Let this in, then take some time to enjoy those feelings of self-kindness and acknowledgement. Doing these steps first will make it much easier to let go of this issue of blame. Now turn your attention to the issue of blame to start to resolve it.

6. Step back to the Inner Coach and say to 'You':
    a. I know this has been something you've felt you couldn't or shouldn't let go of.
    b. But it's hurting you to keep it.

7. Now climb up onto the chair/bed behind the Inner Coach. From this position, you'll review your younger self's decision to hold on to that hurt from the past event. Again, notice how physically stepping up and back increases that sense of distance and perspective even more. From here, you will see it very differently, with much less emotion and more rationality. As you reflect on it from up here, you'll find you can make different choices much more easily. Ask the 'You' over there: 'This doesn't look useful for you anymore - is it Ok to let it go, now?'

8. Return to the 'You' position and notice your answer - it should be 'yes'.*

9. Step back to the chair/bed and ask, 'Is there anything useful that you need to learn from this, that helps your future, before you can let it go completely?'

10. Step back into 'You' and notice your answer. You might be surprised at what comes up from your IW. Take a few deep breaths as you allow yourself to absorb these important learnings into your body, gut, heart, and mind.

11. Finally, reconnect with the Gateway State of Kindness again and feel it flowing through you and anyone else involved. Flowing through those old past events, softening, shrinking, blurring out, and distancing those events. Freeing yourself to step into your life in a new way. Feel how this future feels as you explore it with this sense of ease and flow. Notice how you feel different now.

Some notes on the process:

- Again, If you aren't able to easily or safely access a suitable chair or bed, then you can imagine yourself being one floor above where you are and looking down.

- Some people find it easier to do the process in an upstairs room and imagine seeing the 'You' down there, outside at ground level.

- *As you practice this IWT you may start to apply it to more complex issues. Sometimes in steps 6/7, you may find some sense of resistance, objection, or reluctance to let it go. This is fine, as there will be excellent reasons for this that need to be listened to. Other IWT 17, working with Parts, may resolve this for you, but in cases of trauma or serious adverse events in your past, you may need the help of an experienced practitioner. Remember, IW doesn't mean doing it on your own, part of wisdom is knowing when to seek extra support, and this is something that will be part of the fascinating topics we'll explore in the next chapters.

Having completed this technique, I'd again recommend taking a break for a few minutes after this to let that important work process through your mind, brain, and body. Ideally, go for a walk in nature if you can, as this will help the change process.

'Holding onto anger is like swallowing poison and expecting someone else to die.'

CHAPTER 15: SHIFT - PASSIVE AND ACTIVE

In the previous chapter, we noticed an issue arises when we really want things like a boss, the past, or our partner to change. This often results in us feeling frustrated and annoyed. This is because those three things are ones that, unfortunately, we don't actually have the power to change - although most of us have probably tried, unsuccessfully, to get others to change at some point.

This issue highlights an IW concept that has been central to so much of my work over the last 30 years. It's the concept of 'Passive and Active' and discovering it has been life-changing for so many.

Let me explain what I mean by the terms Passive and Active, in this context.

- 'Passive' describes situations that we have no power to change, such as the weather, the past, traffic, or indeed other people's behaviour.
- 'Active' describes things we can do something about, things we can make choices about, these include our diet, how much we exercise, whom we vote for, and what we think or do.

This useful distinction identifies those things that are worth spending time on changing and those we need to find ways to accept and deal with differently.

THE PASSIVE PROBLEM

The problem arises when we mistakenly think a situation is:

- One of those things we can't do anything about, so, we are passive to it.
- But in fact, this is a misunderstanding. We have forgotten that we can influence it and that it's something we can actively make a difference to.

Think of it as if we have two filing cabinets. One marked 'things you can do something about', and the other, 'nothing you can do about this'. Filing something in the wrong place generally causes a heap of trouble.

Imagine the problems that arise with misfiling 'bills I've paid' and 'bills I need to pay' or 'poisonous snakes to avoid' and 'non-venomous ones to hang out with'.

A simple example of how this 'passive misfiling' affects us can be seen in the statement 'I am stressed by the world economy'. This statement makes it seem that our stress is *directly caused by* the world economy, and:

1. As the world economy is something we can't directly influence or change (we are passive to it).
2. It follows that we are destined to continue to feel stressed as long as the world economy is in trouble.

However, this set of statements and the consequences that follow from them, are not completely true and need closer examination.

Statement 1 is correct; the world economy is something that we are passive to.

However, statement 2 isn't quite right. Although the world economy may be in trouble currently, sometimes we feel stressed about it and sometimes we don't. This may be because our attention is focused on other things, like, for example, when we're immersed in the company of great friends, engaged in the fabulous movie we're watching, etc. In these moments, we may experience happiness rather than stress, even though the world economy is still in bad shape.

So, it's clear that the original statement, 'our stress is *directly caused by* the world economy' isn't quite accurate. This cause (world economy) and effect (stress) relationship isn't as straightforward as it implies. We need a better way to explain this connection between the world economy and our stress levels.

When we were at the movie, or enjoying ourselves and focused on that, we were activating certain parts of our neurology, releasing neurotransmitters and hormones, and as a result, we felt happy.

However, when we turn our attention to the problems of the world economy and start to ruminate and worry about it, we switch on different neurology, neurotransmitters, and hormones, producing feelings of stress.

So, it's more accurate to say that when we were feeling stressed about the world economy, it was because we were switching on neurological and physiological processes in our body - it was **us,** not the world economy, producing the feelings of stress. And when we were feeling happy, even though the world economy was still in trouble, it was **us** producing that happiness.

This identifies that there is some unintentional involvement from us in the creation of the stress, and that it is not caused *directly* by the world economy. It's caused by the way we are thinking about the world economy.

To make this concept simple to use in practice, I designed a verb called dû[27]. Using the verb dû allows us to shift these types of inaccurate passive statements, where we mistakenly feel like we have no power (in this case, no power over whether we are stressed or not), into active ones, where we regain the sense that we can exert some influence (again, in this case, over how stressed we feel). Another way to think of it is, using 'dû' flags the things we were about to incorrectly file in the 'nothing you can do about this' filing cabinet and reminds us to refile them into the 'things you can do something about' filing cabinet.

IWT 12: Using Dû
To see how it works and what it feels like to use it, let's apply it to the statement:

- 'I am stressed by the world economy'.
Many people would naturally place this statement in the 'nothing you can do about this' filing cabinet. But from the earlier evaluation, we know that's the wrong place for it. The statement has two parts - 'the stress' and 'the world economy'. Which sections are we truly passive

to?

The second section, 'the world economy', is separate from us, it is not within our power to change it, so we are passive to this bit. The first section, 'the stress', which is occurring within us is, however, something we can have influence over, so this is where we apply 'dû'. This shifts it to:

- 'I am dûing stress about the world economy.'

Say the statement out loud twice, once without the du and notice how the 'dû' version feels different.

Using dû reminds us that, although that's how it can feel, the stress isn't coming from the world economy, it's coming from us. Notice how this flags this for filing in the 'things you can do something about' filing cabinet. As it's us producing the stress, *unconsciously and unintentionally*, then it is something we can do something about - if we have some de-stressing skills to hand, like the IWT.

DÛ AND DO

So, you're probably wondering why there's a û in dû? It's there to distinguish it from the normal verb 'do', because, although they both have some similar meanings, 'dû' is different in some important ways. 'Do' means 'to perform an action or achieve something' and has a sense of 'choosing to *do it* on purpose' and may lead to a sense of being 'at fault or to blame'.

The 'û' of dû instead distinguishes that this is happening at an **u**nintentional and **u**nconscious level. This avoids the verb do's sense of being 'at fault or to blame'. Instead, 'dû' identifies it as something that you have just learnt to do over time so effectively that now it runs automatically, as a result of neuroplasticity.

So dû restores our active role - identifying that we are involved in some way in the issue (after all, if I am stressed, the stress is occurring in *my* nervous system), and emphasising that this is occurring at an *unconscious and unintentional* level. And there's further good news.

It also reminds us that as **we** are **dûing it**, we also have *influence* to do something different instead and can change what happens next.

Using this new verb produces some fascinating and instant MAPP shifts, and achieves this in several ways:

Awakening: The unfamiliarity of saying 'I am dûing stress' is designed to 'sound wrong'. This helps us identify and question our sense of having no power to create a solution.

Options: This new awareness is accompanied by the realisation: 'if I am 'dûing' it, then maybe I can stop dûing it and do something else'

Distance: The recognition that I am dûing it removes the sense of it just happening to me and that I'm a passive bystander in the situation. Instead, it provides a feeling of distance and perspective from the experience (remember how important that is from the Inner Coaching skills sections) which builds our sense of having some power to change it

Temporariness: Using dû reminds us that this is a temporary and changeable process that will end. It is a kind of shorthand for 'I'm currently switching on stress, at the moment, without meaning to'. Other researchers, including Dweck's work on growth mindsets and Seligman's research into optimism [30,31] have also identified how essential this sense of temporariness is for change and happiness.

Cause and effect: The dû highlights the cause-and-effect error suggested by 'the world economy *made me* stressed'. This new understanding of how they aren't directly linked means:

- The world economy can still be in trouble and out of our control.
- But our stress doesn't have to be.

Identity: Using dû also helps resolve the effect of damaging self-comments, such as 'I am a depressive', 'I am hopeless', or 'I'm a lazy dreamer'. These are known as 'identity statements' as they incorrectly describe an issue as an unchangeable part of who we are. The dû identifies them instead as behaviours that we've become well-practised at dûing. This can make a huge difference to how we approach resolving the issue. Notice how more solvable the depression feels when we move from it 'I am a depressive' to 'I dû depression much of the time'. There is still clearly work to do, but now it feels that it's possible. It is moved from the passive filing cabinet of 'nothing you can do to change this' to the active 'things you can do something about'.

That a single word can address all these issues, in a moment, shows how valuable it is, and since its development, over 25 years ago, it's been used by tens of thousands of people aged 6 and up and has been translated into multiple languages (see duing.org for more).

Using dû identifies that we are not powerless and that there are options available to us. This is the essential first step of change. Then, armed with the IWT, and any other skills we have, we can begin to find solutions to our issues.

SERENITY

The importance of using our influence in this way has been identified as a key part of developing wisdom by many philosophers throughout history. One of my favourites is the prayer by Reinhold Niebuhr, which captures the ideas behind dû brilliantly and simply. The adapted version that follows has three simple lines:

Let me find

1. The serenity to accept the things I cannot change.
2. The courage to change the things I can.
3. And the wisdom to know the difference between these two.

These three lines teach the IW of understanding responsibility, blame, fault, and influence, and Passive and Active.

The first line identifies how it's vital to recognise those things that we can't change and to choose not to put any energy into them. Although this is something that many of us forget from time to time. Have you noticed how often people put all their energy into trying to change things they can't change? They're dûing annoyed with the rain when they planned to have a barbecue or the traffic when they're late.

The second calls us to be responsible, take action, and change the things that we can influence.

The third reminds us to use our IW to correctly distinguish which filing cabinet a thing belongs in 'nothing you can do about this' or 'things you can do something about'.

When the thing we are dûing annoyed about is something that we are truly passive to, like the weather, traffic, other people's behaviours, or opinions, etc., then there's no point in putting energy into complaining about it, wishing it away or trying to 'fix' it. Obviously, we just don't have the power to change these things.

Freeing ourselves from trying to fix these things allows us to use our energy instead to shift the thing that we have the most power to change - our response to those situations. That includes what thoughts, actions and communications we are dûing.

Notice today how many people you see are dûing not applying this simple three-line suggestion for living, and how it makes life harder for them as a result. I highly recommend making sure you're not part of that group because it's one of the best ways to dû wasting energy and life.

PRACTISING DÛ

You probably spotted my use of dû in this previous section as in 'dûing annoyed with the traffic'. You may have noticed how, although it felt a bit odd, it made the sentences more accurate, as it's not the traffic that's annoying, it's you generating/responding/creating or, more simply, dûing annoyed at the traffic.

Now it's your turn to use dû. To get familiar with using the new verb, we'll begin with some simple examples of statements that have been misfiled into the passive 'there's nothing you can do about this' filing cabinet. The keywords in *italics* will help you recognise these types of statements in the future. You can also substitute any of the words in **bold** for ones you find yourself using a lot. Take each one and insert 'dû' and notice how different it feels as a result. Once you've done that, move on to the next chapter, where we'll explore some of the possible answers and their effects.

Exercise
1. I *feel* **stressed.**
2. I *have* **pain.**
3. I *have* **inflammation.**
4. It *is* difficult to **change.**
5. I *can't* **relax.**
6. I *am* an **over-eater/over-thinker/smoker/addict.**

'Dû Identifies That We Are Not Powerless And That There Are Options Available To Us.'

CHAPTER 16: SHIFT - BECOMING AN EXPERT IN USING DÛ

This chapter provides the answers to your dû exercise as well as detailed explanations of how it makes a difference for each scenario. Check below to see how well these fit with your answers. There are a lot of different ways you could have phrased it using dû, but these are the most common ones.

1. **I am stressed - I am dûing stress.**

   As in the example of the world economy in the previous chapter, the use of dû reminds us that the stress is the result of the way we are using our brain and body and therefore something we can influence and switch off.

2. **I have pain - I am dûing pain.**

   When we experience pain, it certainly feels like it's a real 'thing' but researchers have found that it doesn't work that way at all. Pain is not a 'thing' that can be weighed, bottled, or observed. Instead, it's a process. It's the result of a series of signals being sent along nerves within your nervous system. Once those signals reach certain parts of your brain, it decides if it is going to interpret them as pain or not. This kind of brain-based decision-making happens all the time. When we put on clothes in the morning, we feel their touch and pressure against our skin immediately, and then after a while, our brain will just switch off those signals because they're no longer important. This highlights the process nature of nerve signals and pain. Pain is not a static thing, it is something that comes and goes, and stops and starts. Therefore, using dû is a much more appropriate and accurate way of explaining what is happening when we experience pain. It also allows us to recognise that if we are dûing pain then this is something that we could influence, whether by resting, applying ice, or using some of the techniques in this book to shift how our neurology is processing those signals.

3. **I have inflammation - I am dûing inflammation.**

Similarly to pain, inflammation, which appears to be a noun, a 'thing', is actually a verb, 'a process'. It involves a complex series of reactions between the affected part of the body and the immune, nervous, and vascular systems. There are changes in blood flow, cells rushing in and signalling to other cells to join them, and chemicals being released to help the recovery process. When you visit your doctor, they don't give you this detailed explanation of what's going on because it would take up too much time. Instead, you're given the shorthand statement 'You have inflammation'. This helps because it's simpler, but it leaves you with the sense that the inflammation is a static 'thing', rather than a changeable process. This is why it's more appropriate to say, 'I am dûing inflammation'. Using dû also reminds us that there are things we can do to affect what happens next. These may include taking medication, or using some of the IWT in this book to calm down the inflammatory process, and speed up the recovery process.

4. **It is difficult to change - I am dûing difficulty around change.**

   The first version suggests it is just difficult to change and there's nothing that can be done about it. The second, dû version, shows up more options. It recognises that the difficulty you've felt in making this change is the result of how you're approaching and thinking about it. If we can approach it differently, based on what we already know about MAPPs and our expectations, then we will find an easier way through this - and after all, who wouldn't want to find life a bit easier?

5. **I can't relax - I am dûing tense/not relaxed. Or I'm dûing it's impossible to relax.**

   This example is similar to #1. It reminds us that we are involved in the process of tension or relaxation. It is not an absolute, fixed lifetime experience (notice it's saying I can NEVER relax, see Chapter 12 on beliefs) but something that comes and goes and that we do have influence over.

125

6. **I am an over-eater/over-thinker/smoker/addict - I am dûing over-eating/over-thinking/smoking/addiction much of the time, or I am dûing eating/thinking/smoking/taking drugs a lot.**

These kinds of 'I am' identity statements, which we saw in the previous chapter, are very powerful. This is because they suggest that this is WHO we are, it's part of our make-up or nature and therefore unchangeable, rather than something that we are currently dûing.

The use of dû switches the focus from having to 'change our whole nature or personality' to the simpler task of finding ways to stop these behaviours. Notice how this helps to reduce how much work it feels might be required to change this situation. This, in turn, makes that change feel more possible. The importance of this shift is backed up by research. A randomised controlled trial using dû and many of the approaches in this book helped people resolve a range of habits, including substance use issues, more effectively than the usual treatment routes [1].

We can see from these examples just how much power this small shift to using dû can provide. From now on, I'd encourage you to try out your new dû language skills on yourself to see how it changes things.

I'd also like to emphasise the importance of Self-Kindness, the ability to be nice to ourselves regardless of how well we are performing, when using dû. It can be easy to dû being hard on ourselves for running unhelpful patterns that we know don't serve us. However, an intrinsic part of dû is the sense of not being to blame for the patterns we run. They are the result of a younger version of ourselves' best attempt to deal with life, something you'll cover in great depth in Chapter 19 on working with 'Parts'. Any self-criticism or judgement is not only not nice, it's harmful as it increases the amount of negative neurology that we are activating, causing us even more problems. So, make sure you practice the Gateway State of Self-Kindness as you use this new language tool.

IWT 13: When Do I Use Dû?

I chose the examples above because they are good illustrations of simple, mistaken passive statements. Spotting them in real life takes a little more focus. It involves a three-stage process, that we saw at work in our first example 'I am stressed by the world economy'.

1. **Awareness.** The first step is to notice key signs that it is time to use this process.
   a. Watch for when you find yourself feeling limited in what you can do, what the future holds, or are describing a problem you feel stuck with (**I am stressed**).
   b. Certain keywords, that were highlighted in italics in the previous exercise, will also alert you to use this process of clarifying in which filing cabinet we should be placing this statement:
      i. I am.
      ii. It is.
      iii. I have.
      iv. I feel.
      v. I can't.
      vi. It made me.
2. **Evaluate.** Next, we evaluate the statement for:
   a. Things we are actually passive to (in our example, **the world economy**).
   b. Things we have mistakenly thought we were passive to (**the stress**) - these are often 'states'.
3. **Dû.** Take the section from 2b (**the stress**) that we mistakenly thought we were passive to and use dû to re-establish your sense of influence (**I'm dûing stress**).

You can follow this process through another example:

'I am nervous at interviews'

1. **Awareness**. This is limiting, describes a stuck problem and uses the keywords 'I am x'.
2. **Evaluate.**
    a. You are passive about having to go to interviews to get a job/university place etc. You may not like them but if you want to get that job, you have to be interviewed.
    b. Nervousness, however, is a state and so this is something you could influence.
3. **Dû.** This becomes 'I am dûing nervous at interviews (at the moment)'. Notice how it now feels like there is something you can do about this instead of just having to suffer it.

USAGE IN THE BOOK

Now that we share this new, more accurate, and wiser way of using language, let's use it throughout the book. You'll notice it showing up to identify where we are unconsciously and unintentionally involved in the creation of thoughts and feelings. So instead of writing 'when you feel stressed', I will change it to 'when you are dûing stress'. The only exception will be when I'm giving examples of the kind of passive misfiling we often hear. This serves several purposes. First, it makes the sentence more accurate in terms of describing what's going on. Second, when you first start to use it, it will probably sound a bit odd. This oddness will remind us that we have a choice in that situation. Third, through neuroplasticity, the more you practise and experience the verb, the more familiar it will become, and the more you'll start to use it in your language and your thoughts... and that will be truly revolutionary.

One word of warning. Don't use dû on other people. So, if somebody says, 'I'm really annoyed with you', avoid saying 'I think you're dûing annoyed with me' as that is likely to irritate them even further. You can, of course, explain the dû concept to people who want to know about it and start to use it in your conversations together. It will make life better - but only if you use it with those who want to be part of this revolution in thinking about language and influence.

Next Steps In Dû

There's a common passive statement that follows the pattern of 'something **made me** feel an unpleasant state', such as, 'My boss **made me** angry'. The trouble with this pattern is that it can really feel like 'our boss' did actually '**make us** angry'. However, it's useful to resolve this, as dûing anger often has damaging consequences. It can cause us to respond in unthoughtful ways that may make a situation worse and is linked to a wide range of negative emotional and physical consequences, including affecting interpersonal relationships, poor lung function, delayed wound healing, and depression[32–35].

Avoiding this kind of trap is such an important part of IW that we'll explore it in depth in the next chapter, along with some IWT that support how we can deal with these kinds of situations differently.

CHAPTER 17: SHIFT - MY BOSS MADE ME ANGRY

HE MADE ME...

Our first stop in working through this issue is to become aware of the phrase 'made me'. You can hear this way of talking about emotions and upset in conversations in many bars, cafés, families, and workplaces. It follows the structure:

- This [event/behaviour of someone else] made me [feel this way].

This phrase and its close cousin, 'He **caused me** to feel x' are so familiar and feel like 'true' depictions of what happened that we need to spend some time unpacking them. Identifying why these kinds of statements catch us out, and how to resolve them are your next steps on your journey to building great IW.

TRIGGERS AND INVITATIONS

Let's apply the 3-step process from IWT 16 to the statement, 'My boss made me angry':

1. Awareness - we can notice the key phrase - 'Made me'.
2. Evaluate - Next, we evaluate the statement for:
   a. Things we are actually passive to, in this case, 'My boss'. Who is doing 'some behaviour'.
   b. Things we have mistakenly thought we were passive to - these are often 'states'. In this case, it's 'Me, and I am angry'.

Splitting it up in this way helps us recognise that these two things are not as linked as we first thought. You might be ready for step 3, 'Using Dû' on this right now, but from experience, I've found a little further exploration of MAPPs, Triggers, and Invitations is often useful first.

It is still true that the boss was doing something that encouraged us to dû angry. But we can also see that we had a part to play in this too. We responded to their behaviour by dûing angry. Granted, it doesn't feel that way in that moment, it feels as if our boss triggered our response.

But if we can just view it in slow motion, we can see there are some steps between the boss's behaviour and our anger. So, what's going on here? This is the tricky territory of Triggers and Invitations.

The word 'Trigger' is often used to describe situations when it feels like an external force has set off a response inside of you. Examples of this include 'that triggered my anxiety' or 'she triggered me'. These phrases are attempting to explain how a person rapidly felt themselves getting into/dûing a deeply unsettling state of mind after some event or situation. It happens so quickly it feels like a one-step process:

MAPP 1
1. The other person did something/something external happened to me, and it triggered me.

However, due to how quickly we start dûing the feelings, some of the steps seem to speed by so fleetingly that they are hard to spot. If we can slow down the process, we'll see it is a bit more complicated and runs like this:

MAPP 2
1. The other person did something/something external happened to me.
2. We processed that information in some way, very rapidly and often unconsciously. This processing is often influenced by negative past experiences, which seem similar in some way to the current experience.
3. This generates an unpleasant set of neurological and hormonal responses, causing us to feel physical and emotional upset.
4. We report this as 'it triggered me'.

Which MAPP is more accurate?

Many people experience being 'triggered' by recalling a past event or one in the future which can make us dû upset. Here, point 1 doesn't occur, as there is no external person or event. The pattern starts at Point 2. This suggests that MAPP 2 more accurately explains how we rapidly move from dûing ok to 'triggered' and identifies the key components driving that response are not the other person but what we've been unintentionally thinking.

We can also apply the Simple, Big Question, from IWT 8, asking, 'Which MAPP is most useful?'

Let's compare the effects of experiencing the world through these two MAPPS.

If we understand the world through MAPP 1 that 'people trigger us' it limits our options for resolving the problem. The solutions all involve addressing Point 1 'The other person did something/something external happened to me' and fall into two categories. The first option is to find a way to stop the other people from acting in that 'triggering' way, but as we know, it's difficult to get others to change what they do. The second is to avoid places or people where those things might happen. Neither of these options is easy to achieve, and both encourage the idea that we are passive and powerless, that we can't cope with others, and that we can't live in the world as it is.

If we see the world through MAPP 2 things become a bit easier to deal with.

Point 1 - in both MAPPS we have no influence over this.

Point 2 - 'We processed that information in some way', this is where, with help, we could shift from this familiar but unhelpful pathway and find different ways to respond to the events in Point 1. Or, to put it simply, to find a way to stop dûing that response and do something else. (If you're wondering, that second 'do' has no û as it is a conscious and intentional choice). If we can find a way to access more useful neurology at Point 2, we will avoid the pattern of continuing to Points 3 and 4 and of dûing 'triggered'.

A great way to achieve this is to consider the idea of 'Invitations'. Some people's behaviours and conversations provide an easy opportunity for us to dû recalling prior bad experiences. We know we can't change how people behave and will bump into people like this from time to time, so how can we deal with it differently? What if we saw it as an invitation?

Imagine someone inviting you to a party and they let you know you were completely free to choose to come or not. From their description of the party, you discover, for example, it will take hours to get there; it's a meat BBQ and you're a vegetarian; it's focused around watching people play chess - something you don't enjoy; the people hosting it are nudists - and that's not your kind of thing; they love the kind of music that you don't like; basically, it will be a party that has little to offer you. As invitations differ from obligations, in that you are free to decline or accept them - would you go to this party? With this knowledge about the party, you would probably politely decline the invitation.

What if you took people's tricky behaviours, 'She looked at me in that way', 'he said something mean' etc., as invitations to dû deeply upset?

If you could find a way to see it like an invitation to that dreadful party that you wouldn't enjoy, and you felt free to accept or decline their invitation to join them in that predictably awful experience, how would that change things?

Exercise
Take a minute and think about which people in your life often 'invite' you to 'dû a bad state' when you're with them?

And what might be the benefits to you of declining those requests?

THE WISDOM OF FISH
My dad was a keen fisherman. He would spend hours watching the water for fish, choosing the right bait, and casting it onto the water so it was just in front of the fish's mouth. The bait, in this case, was some feathers and a hook, designed to look, to the fish, like a tasty fly. He was the kind of fisherman who threw the fish back in the water after he caught them, and as a result, there were some fish in that river that had been caught and released many times. These, he said, were the most difficult fish to catch. He would cast 'the fly' so it was just above their

mouth, in the best place for them to bite on it, and they would swim up to it and have a look at it. And they'd think to their wise fishy selves, 'Wait a minute - I remember this fly. This is the one that caught me and dragged me out of the water last time. I didn't like that, so I'm not going to be fooled by this twice.' And sagely, they'd swim away.

So, it seems that these fish are slightly wiser than we are, as how many times have we fallen for the same bait? How many times have we been hooked out of our nice gently flowing river and thrown into dûing unpleasant feelings as a result of being lured by somebody else's invitation to 'bite'? How many times have we found ourselves in the same argument, lashing out or responding like an annoyed teenager and regretting it later... Maybe we need to learn from the wisdom of fish and get wise and avoid the hooks we've been caught with so many times before.

CAN WE REALLY CHANGE HOW WE RESPOND?
People often ask me, 'Is it really possible to change my response and to treat these things as invitations? Surely, when someone does something nasty, you have to respond with upset?' It's a great question, and I often give them this example to help make sense of this.

Imagine Sam is walking down the street and passing a restaurant and sees a family he doesn't know having a meal together. He rushes in and hits one of the men hard on the back, grabs him, and throws him around. How does everyone respond?

You would probably guess that they will be quite annoyed, surprised, shocked, or outraged by Sam's behaviour.

But what if Sam was walking past that restaurant and sees that the man was choking, and nobody knows what to do? He rushes in, hits him on the back, grabs him, and performs the Heimlich manoeuvre to see if he can release the food that is obstructing his airway - it works, and he can breathe again.

How does everybody respond to his very physical intervention? Now they interpret this behaviour in a completely different way, they're thankful for his actions.

This is because it's not so much what happens, as what it means to them. The actions are the same in both scenarios. In the first one, there is no context for Sam's actions, they are interpreted as unpleasant, and in the second, the same actions are seen as life-saving, and something to be grateful for. If we can dû a different response to such an extreme event as this, depending on the context, it highlights that we do have choices about how we respond to events.

You may have had the experience of texting a friend to see how they are, but you don't get a text back in reply. That's unusual. So, you call them. This time, they put the phone down as soon as they hear your voice. So, you email and text again, but you're still not getting any response. You start to dû worry, wondering if something has gone badly wrong with your friendship. Have you done or said something that has upset them? Are they ok? What's going on? The longer this situation continues, the more certain you are that something is wrong. Now you're dûing sad as this friendship seems to be in serious trouble and you're not sure if it can be repaired. Coming back to the idea of maps, your MAPP of how well this friendship is going has now altered. When you see them two days later, they're very pleased to see you. They're so sorry they've been out of contact and tell you about the series of unfortunate events that unfolded over the last few days - their phone had been stolen, their internet has not been working, etc. that explains why you couldn't get hold of them. With this new information, you understand the events in a new way, and your inner map MAPP of the friendship shifts back to how it was before. Suddenly, the sad emotions you've been dûing disappear. It's important to note two things about those emotions. First, they were real feelings caused by the release of neurochemicals and hormones in your brain and body. Second, those chemicals and feelings were generated from a misunderstanding of the situation and based on imagined events (they are avoiding me, they don't like me anymore) that weren't based on what was really happening. When we are dûing those emotions, they feel very powerful, and it feels difficult to step away from them. They don't feel like an invitation at all. But we can see from this example that when we get that new information (the friend's phone was lost rather than that they didn't like us anymore), we can stop dûing those strong feelings in an instant. This identifies how much the emotions we are dûing can change depending on how we are thinking about things.

This opens a central section of IW, the concept that **the meaning of an event is shaped by how you choose to respond to it**. This short sentence is incredibly important to understand, but, as we can see from the sections above, it runs counter to how most people see the world. The word 'choose' is so important here. So often, it really feels like there isn't a choice; that when 'they did that' it *made us* respond in that way. I'm sure we've all felt that. But what if we could pause, see that Invitation, step away from it, and bring that choice into our conscious awareness, rather than dûing our usual response unconsciously and unintentionally?

To develop this aspect of IW we need to build awareness of when we are not responding to things in our wisest way and then make wiser choices to respond in the best way we can. And this brings us back full circle to the central themes of the serenity prayer and the concepts of responsibility, influence, and active and passive. So, the next time you feel someone else has:

- 'Triggered you'
- 'Put you' in a bad state
  - o Reactive.
  - o Angered.
  - o Stressed.
  - o Furious.
  - o Saddened, etc.

Pause for a moment and consider if accepting this *Invitation* is your wisest choice. If not, then we can continue on our journey through the 3-step process.

RESOLVING OUR ANGER ABOUT THE BOSS

As this last important section has taken up a few pages, let's remind ourselves where we got to with, 'My boss made me angry'...

1. Awareness - Notice the key phrase - 'Made me'.
2. Evaluate - Next, we chop up and evaluate the statement for:
    a. Things we are actually passive to - 'My boss'. Who is doing 'some behaviour'.
    b. Things we have mistakenly thought we were passive to - these are often 'states'- 'I am dûing angry'.
3. Applying dû to the phrase in 2b changes it to - My boss did something, and I dîd angry about it. (Dîd is the past tense of dû)

Finally, we have an accurate version of what happened and a route out of our problematic response. Using dû reminds us that, as we can't change the boss, the only person we have real power to change is ourselves. Identifying this means we have taken the first step in resolving the situation, as at this point we regain our power. We can recognise that we are dûing anger and, independent of the boss' behaviour, that it's up to us to recognise our involvement in the creation of our anger and influence what happens.

Having done that, the next steps might involve leaving the job, having a clear, calm chat with your boss about it, raising it with the HR department, ignoring it and getting on with your work or dealing with it for a few more days as he's about to be sacked anyway. Using dû opens the door to so many other options for thinking and responding in a more useful way. When we leave the old 'triggers' MAPP behind, it removes that clash of the inner and outer worlds that in the past has so often knocked us off balance. It frees us up to bring IW to guide us to choose our responses to events, and then we have a chance to design what happens next in our lives.

So, if like many of us, you've found yourself dûing these kinds of patterns, maybe it's time to pause, rethink if that is really working for you, and discover new choices in those old situations.

IWT 14: Given That

Now that we've explored the concepts of taking responsibility and using our influence, even in those situations where it feels unfair to have to do so, we are ready to apply an advanced IWT. 'Given That' IWT brings together so much of what's been covered so far in this book. As a result, I'd recommend spending some time mastering it and then using it on everything you come across, as it produces such powerful change. It's great for resolving areas where we dû feeling stuck or that we're having to work against huge obstacles, long-term difficulties, or challenging behaviours of others.

It does this by combining Inner Coaching with Kindness and an acknowledgement of how it has been to deal with this block. You'll also be meeting a new, extremely powerful question - 'WHO are you going to be as you deal with this?'. This question asks you to consider how you want to show up in this situation and answering this will reconnect you with those aspects of your identity that are exactly what are required to overcome this obstacle. This reminds you that you are a force of nature and that when you channel that empowered inner aspect of who you know yourself to be, you can overcome this. It also introduces how we can incorporate movement in a new way to the now familiar 'Inner Coach' and 'You' patterns you've mastered in the book already.

Begin by taking an issue that you're dûing stuck with. It may often take the form of a complaint, such as:

'I've **tried so hard** to change this in so many ways, but **it just never shifts, and** it feels like **the world is against me** and **I can't see a way through** it.'

Get prepared as before. Arrange the 'You' and 'Inner Coach' as usual. Stand in the 'You' position, making sure there is about 1 metre of space in front of you, and for this IWT, have 2 -3 metres to one side of you (in this example, I'll write the instructions as though it is to your left, but either side is fine) and take 5 deep, easy breaths. As this process has several parts, I'll indicate the end of each section, where you can pause for a few moments, with a solid line _____ to make it easier to follow.

1. In the 'You' position (shown by the dotted-line circle), reconnect with the Gateway State of 'Shift' you accessed in IWT 9 .
2. As before, using this updated diagram as a guide:
   a. Step into the space just in front of you (the solid-line circle) marked 'Inner Coach'.
   b. Then turn around 180 degrees so you are looking back towards the space you were just standing in (as shown by the arrow pointing to the LEFT).

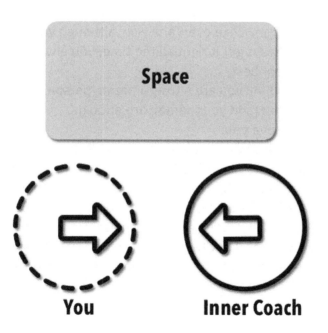

3. Take the role of the Inner Coach. See the 'You' still standing in that dotted-line circle right in front of you - in the 'You' position. Looking directly at the 'You' over there, say out loud, as you did the Self-Kindness IWT 4:
    a. 'I'm so proud of you and all that you have achieved.'
    b. 'Like that time when you...' (List a few things that you know took a lot of effort from you to make happen).
    c. 'I see these qualities in you...' (List them)
    d. 'You're really good at...' (List a few stand-out examples of skills and abilities that you know you have. No one else is listening, so it's ok to say them out loud. Examples include being patient with kids/making fabulous soup/gardening/making friends, etc. but choose YOUR own).
    e. 'And I really like that about you.'
    f. 'I know you've had to deal with some stuff in your life and you always keep going.'
    g. 'I know, like everyone else, although you don't always get it right all the time, you always do your very best.'
    h. 'I think you are a truly amazing person.'
    i. 'You (add your name), are enough'.
    j. 'I love you.'
4. Step back into the 'You' in the dotted-line circle and feel how it feels to hear your Inner Coach say these things to you. Let this in, then take some time to enjoy those feelings of self-kindness and acknowledgement. Doing these steps first will make it much easier to move through the next steps. Now turn your attention to the issue you've been dûing stuck about and start to resolve it by placing it in the 'Space' to your left.

---

5. Step back to the Inner Coach and, pointing to the issue in the 'Space', say to 'You': 'I know this has been something you've found difficult to deal with, and I really get that.'
6. Step back into 'You' and notice how that feels to have your Inner Coach on your side, understanding what's been going on for you.
7. Step back to the Inner Coach, and pointing to the issue in the 'Space' say:
   a. GIVEN THAT, (and repeat the problem statement but with added 'feels like' or 'seems like' phrases to weaken the limiting beliefs you've started to build)
      i. You've **tried so hard** to change this in so many ways.
      ii. But **it *seems like* it just never shifts.**
      iii. And **it feels like the world is against you.**
      iv. And it *feels like* **you can't see a way through** it.
   b. WHO do you want to be as you deal with this?
8. Step back into 'You' and notice your answer. You might be surprised at what comes up from your IW. Take a few deep breaths as you deeply connect with this powerful sense of WHO you can be as you take this on. Allow yourself to absorb this sense of WHO you can be into your body, gut, heart, and mind.

   _____

9. Now that you know WHO you will be as you work through this, step back to the Inner Coach, and pointing to the issue in the 'Space' ask, 'GIVEN ALL THAT WHICH Gateway State, or another state, would help you move through this in the most empowered way?
10. Step back into 'You' and notice which state will be most useful. Take yourself back to a time when you deeply experienced this in the way you've practised throughout the book. Take a few deep breaths as you deeply connect with the powerful state you've chosen. Allow yourself to absorb this feeling into your body, gut, heart, and mind.

11. In a moment, this 'powered up' You and your Inner Coach are going to step together in, and through, that 'Space' that represents the issues you used to dû stuck with. Feeling that state you chose in step 10 and reconnecting with WHO you are going to be, turn towards the 'Space' and step in, and through it. Hear, see, imagine, and feel the presence and support of your Inner Coach walking next to You. Notice how it feels to move in this new way through this area of your life where you used to dû stuck.

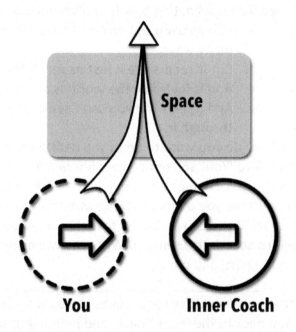

You　　　　　　Inner Coach

12. Step beyond it, to the head of the arrow, with your Inner Coach beside you, and look back. How does it feel to see and experience this change?
13. Staying here, connect with the Gateway State of Kindness again and feel it flowing through you and anyone else involved. Flowing through those old places where you used to dû stuck, but in a completely new way, with these new states and this new sense of who you are. Notice how

> you feel differently now. How does having that right now shift your experience of the world?

Notes:

Step 5: This is the acknowledgement step. You could also phrase it with dû: 'I know this is something you've been dûing difficulty about how to deal with it, and I really get that.'

Step 7a: Using the phrases 'feels like' or 'seems like' helps shift your MAPP. They reduce the sense of permanence of these issues while acknowledging that you've been finding them hard.

Step 10: You may often find that more than one state is required. Either choose a moment from your past that has both of those states present, or choose two separate moments and connect with them one at a time.

Step 11: In this step, you are adding a new set of movements to the IWT. The previous steps prepared us to move through the old stuckness with some positive new neurology all fired up, which shifts how that aspect of our lives feels. You are also moving 'beyond' the stuckness - both physically and by going forward in time to when it has been resolved and turning around and seeing it from the other side. This powerful change in perspective (remember that from the coaching qualities) changes our distance in both location and time and provides another transformational way to shift how we feel about events that we were dûing stuck with.

You can repeat this IWT as often as you need to for whatever blocks you find yourself dealing with. It is such a powerful technique, as you will discover the more you use it.

From time to time, you may find another aspect of the same issue showing up at a later date. If so, just calmly apply the same process to it. It's just a sign of how well that old neuroplastic training that built those blocking pathways worked. As we now know, neuroplasticity is always on, so retraining your brain each time will result in these new patterns becoming your default way of thinking.

ENDING

In this section on Shift, we've explored how Shift helps us see the world differently, let go of old beliefs and MAPPS about ourselves, and the need to blame others or focus on the past. We discovered how we can re-empower ourselves by shifting our language and moving from a 'Triggers' based MAPP to an 'Invitations' one, choosing our responses to events rather than being compelled into old, outdated habits and behaviours.

We explored the advanced 'Given That' process, which combines many elements of IW we've discovered so far. This provides a flexible and robust tool suitable for dealing with so many of life's issues. Try it out on everything you can and see what kind of extraordinary changes show up as a result.

Our next section on IW is exploring the Gateway State of Transformation. It's a particular type of Shift, which will bring us some extra wisdom and some incredibly important IWT.

'Given That...Who Are You Going To Be?'

CHAPTER 18: TRANSFORMATION

TRANSFORMATION

The Gateway State of Transformation is a special type of Shift that occurs occasionally in our lives. We've seen that Shift describes the wonderful experience of seeing something change and a new road opening up ahead - whether the stimulus for that was good or bad. Transformation is a little different. It's the result of:

1. Taking a journey through some difficult times and coming out the other side.
2. Or by identifying some negative behaviour, worldview, or habit and resolving it.
   And, by going through that process, discovering something profound and life-changing.

So, it's turning something difficult into something incredibly valuable. Whether the changes occur through route 1 or 2, they are similarly Transformational. A good way to remember this is to think 'disaster into diamonds', as often these experiences spark a sense of Transformation at an incredibly deep level.

Route 1 is often described as Post Traumatic Growth (PTG)[36]. This is the new sense of purpose and change that people discover after moving through and past serious life events such as trauma, recovering from a serious illness, bereavement, divorce, narrowly escaping death, etc. They often report feeling as if they are starting a new life, almost as if they have been given a second chance. You can often identify its presence by the person being surprised to find themselves saying:

> *'It feels weird to be saying this because it was such a horrible experience. But I'm kind of grateful for the fact it happened. I don't think I would have found my way into this new phase in my life in any other way.*
>
> *I needed something this strong and this difficult to wake me up to a new future. So, as bizarre as it sounds, I'm thankful that I*

had... (cancer, lost my leg, nearly died, etc.) - although, of course, I wish I could have learned this in a slightly easier way. But with the way I was heading before this, I just don't think I would have discovered this in any other way.'

This is something I have heard so often in my work, yet I still dû surprise at hearing how such a severe challenge can produce so much positive change.

Similarly, Transformational effects result from the types of changes identified in Route 2.

Independent of the route to this sense of Transformation, it often uncovers new pathways into their future, a new sense of purpose, and shifts their views of themselves, the world, and what is truly important. It also often opens up new understandings for them on a range of the big questions in life. These can include new perspectives on life's meaning, how they deal with life's fragility or its inevitable end, what goes after that, our sense of soul or spark, our place in the vastness of the universe or the aeons of human history, and so on.

In these next chapters, we'll be exploring this Gateway State, looking at some of the MAPP shifts that it produces, and introducing some new IWT that have developed from it.

IWT 15: Reconnect with Transformation
Set aside 5 minutes for this technique, which will reconnect you to some powerful moments of Transformation in your past. Get prepared as before.

1. Allow your mind to drift back through the thousands of memories that you've collected throughout your life, to a time when you had this powerful sense of Transformation. As described above, there are many types of moments that may stand out for you, either:
    a. Choose one that really calls to you from your personal experience, where you moved through

and beyond some severe challenge and experienced something new and life-enhancing as a result.

    b. Or you may be inspired by hearing about someone else's journey and connecting with how they experienced that sense of transformation in their lives. There are so many examples: Maybe it's Gandhi's experience of racism and oppression that made him determined to overthrow British rule in India; or Oprah Winfrey, who transformed her experiences of childhood neglect and abuse into her passion for helping those with mental health issues and a history of trauma; or a charity you support that exists as a consequence of the founder's personal experience of dealing with life's challenges; or maybe it's someone you know who has been through some difficult situation and it's been life-changing, in a positive way, for them.

2. Whichever type of memory you choose, fully connect with, and immerse yourself in that experience. As you step fully into it, notice what you can:

    a. **See** around you.

    b. **Hear** what's going on around you as well as what's going on inside your head.

    c. **Feel** physically (such as your breathing and posture, the temperature on your skin, etc.) and emotionally.

3. If that feeling and sensation were to have a colour, what colour would it be? Let that colour flow throughout your body, becoming even stronger and deeper with each breath.

4. Feel that passion and unstoppable force of connecting with your experience of Transformation, let it flow through:

    a. Relationships, communications, and the places you go to.

    b. Your talents and abilities, actions, and behaviours.

    c. The way you spend your time and energy.

    d. Other beliefs you have about your future and who you really are.

    e. Your ability to show up for others and make an even bigger difference to the things that are deeply important to you.

5. Having experienced this powerful Gateway State of Transformation take a few moments to consider where it might be useful to connect with it in your life.

FAILURE OR FEEDBACK?

One key element linked to IW and the Gateway State of Transformation is how we deal with setbacks and obstacles. In any new adventure, such as starting a job, project, health change, relationship, or reading this book, there will be some things that seem to flow easily and other situations or events where you find yourself dûing confused or stuck.

There are two responses we could have to this second type of event.

The first is an, 'It's a failure' response. We may tell ourselves, 'This isn't working, I can't do this, why did I even bother?'. However, dûing this interpretation that 'this is a failure' doesn't help us much. It can lead to us to giving up and walking away, and maybe justifying our response with mutterings of 'it was stupid, why did I even waste my time with that ridiculous thing.' You know the kind of thing...

Thinking of it as a failure is also not particularly accurate because it suggests it *all* went wrong, *nothing* good came of it, *nothing* was learnt, and it was *completely* pointless. We've met these italicised words before in Chapter 12 on identifying the presence of limiting beliefs.

The second way of responding to this kind of experience is to see it as 'feedback'.

Take anything that you've labelled as a 'failure', and see if it fits this 'feedback focused' description:

- You had an expectation of how something would turn out.
- And, it didn't turn out as you had hoped.

This way of seeing it is much more useful. It strips away the emotional judgements that come bundled with dûing a sense of failure. Now, instead of 'disaster' we start to see the results simply as useful 'data'. This data provides accurate information on what did and didn't work. Using this to adjust our approach in similar situations helps us get better results next time.

Here are two examples where people use this approach.

With the rise in online shopping many have had the experience of ordering some clothes or shoes, and, sometimes when they arrive, the colour or fit isn't as you hoped. You take this as simple feedback, send the items back for a different size or colour, or maybe look elsewhere. We don't see this as a failure, it's just useful information or feedback.

Computer gamers often find that the first few times they try to complete a level, they don't succeed. So, they restart the game and try different ideas. They know that with enough practice, learning from each unsuccessful attempt and adapting as required, they will get through it.

What if we applied this sense of 'feedback' to the things we have been dûing 'failure' about? The next IWT walks you through *how* to do exactly that.

IWT 16: Failure Into Feedback

Get prepared as before. Arrange with the 'You' and 'Inner Coach' as usual. Stand in the 'You' position, making sure there is about 1 metre of space in front of you, and, as we did in 'Given That' IWT 14, have 2 -3 metres to one side of you (in this example, I'll write the instructions as though it is to your left, but either side is fine) and take 5 deep, easy breaths. As this process has several parts, I'll indicate the end of each section, where you can pause for a few moments, with a solid line _____ to make it easier to follow.

Take something you've been dûing 'failure' about recently.

1. In the 'You' position (shown by the dotted-line circle), reconnect with the Gateway States of Transformation and Kindness you previously accessed in IWT 4 and 15
2. As before, using this updated diagram as a guide:
    a. Step into the space just in front of you (the solid-line circle) marked 'Inner Coach'.
    b. Then turn around 180 degrees so you are looking back towards the space you were just standing in (as shown by the arrow pointing to the LEFT).

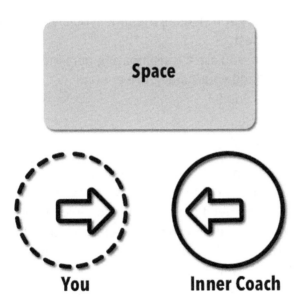

You   **Inner Coach**

3. Take the role of the Inner Coach as before and looking directly at the 'You' over there, say out loud, as you did in the Self-Kindness IWT 4:
    a. I'm so proud of you and all that you have achieved.'

b. 'Like that time when you...' (List a few things that you know took a lot of effort from you to make happen).

c. 'I see these qualities in you...' (List them)

d. 'You're really good at...' (List a few stand-out examples of skills and abilities that you know you have. No one else is listening, so it's ok to say them out loud. Examples include being patient with kids/making fabulous soup/gardening/making friends, etc. but choose YOUR own).

e. 'And I really like that about you.'

f. 'I know you've had to deal with some stuff in your life and you always keep going.'

g. 'I know, like everyone else, although you don't always get it right all the time, you always do your very best.'

h. 'I think you are a truly amazing person.'

i. 'You (add your name), are enough'.

j. 'I love you.'

---

4. Step back into the 'You' in the dotted-line circle and feel how it feels to hear your Inner Coach say these things to you. Let this in, then take some time to enjoy those feelings of self-kindness and acknowledgement. Doing these steps first will make it much easier to move through the next steps. Now turn your attention to the issue you've been dûing 'failure' about and start to resolve it by placing it in the 'Space' to your left.

5. Step back to the Inner Coach and point to the issue in the 'Space' and say to 'You': 'I know this has been something you've found difficult to deal with, and I really get that.'

6. Step back into 'You' and notice how that feels to have your Inner Coach on your side, understanding what's been going on for you.

7. Step back to the Inner Coach and point to the issue in the 'Space' and say:
   a. GIVEN THAT (and repeat the problem 'failure' statement but with added 'feel like' or 'seems like' phrases):
      i. You *feel like* you've **tried so hard** to change this in so many ways
      ii. But **it *seems like* it just never shifts**
      iii. And it *feels like* **you can't see a way through** it.
   b. Ask, 'If you knew then what you know now, how would you approach this differently?'
8. Step back into 'You' and notice your answer. You might be surprised at what comes up from your IW. Continue to step between the Inner Coach, where you ask each of the following 'failure into feedback' questions, and the 'You' as you answer them:
   a. 'What is useful to learn from this experience?'
   b. 'How can you get different results in the future?'
   c. 'What skills do you need to develop more to deal with this more effectively next time?'
   d. 'Who do you need to be to deal with this?'

   ---

9. Then as the Inner Coach ask, 'What Gateway State, or other state, would help you move through this in the most empowered way?'
10. Step back into 'You' and notice which state will be most useful. Take yourself back to a time when you deeply experienced this in the way you've practised throughout the book. Take a few deep breaths as you deeply connect with the powerful state you've chosen. Allow yourself to absorb this feeling into your body, gut, heart, and mind.
11. In a moment this 'powered up' 'You' and your Inner Coach are going to step together in, and through, that 'Space' that represents the issues you used to dû stuck with. Feeling that state you chose in step 10 and reconnecting

with WHO you are going to be, turn towards the 'Space' and step in, and through it. Hear, see, imagine, and feel the presence and support of your Inner Coach walking next to you. Notice how it feels to move in this new way through this area of your life where you used to dû stuck.

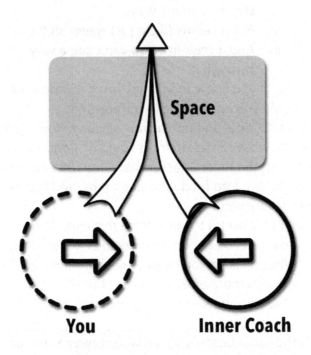

12. Step beyond it, to the head of the arrow, with your Inner Coach beside you, and look back, how does it feel to see and experience this change?

13. Staying there, reconnect with the Gateway State of Kindness again and feel it flowing through you and anyone else involved. Flowing through those old places where you used to dû stuck and giving you a new healing perspective on those moments. Flowing into your future with these new states and a bigger, kinder sense of who you are. Notice how you feel different now.

Notes

Step 3: Keeping this feeling fresh and authentic is so important. If you sense that because you've done this section a few times now that you're just 'saying' these words rather than meaning them, change the words and examples until it feels like you genuinely mean it.

Step 5: You can use the dû here and say 'I know this has been something you've been dûing difficulty about, and I really get that'.

Step 7 or 8: If you find yourself still dûing cross or upset about the event then you can get more perspective and distance by using the chair/bed position just behind the Inner Coach (see IWT 8 for a reminder of this step).

Use this IWT anytime you find yourself dûing hopeless, stuck or failure. Being able to switch from a focus of failure into one of feedback is simply a skill, but one that many people haven't had much experience of. Practising this develops the neuroplastic pathways of IW and deepens our connection with the Gateway State of Transformation.

In the next sections, we'll be exploring how we can directly encourage the type of change found in transformational experiences such as post-traumatic growth. You'll be discovering a fascinating and in-depth ITW, called 'Working with Parts' that transforms old habits, limiting beliefs, inner conflicts and hurts into something completely new, wonderful and life-changing.

'Failure, just means we had a particular expectation about something, and it didn't turn out quite as we hoped.'

CHAPTER 19: WORKING WITH 'PARTS'

Have you ever noticed yourself saying, 'Part of me wants to do with this', for example, to be calm, 'but another Part of me seems to be determined to do the opposite', for example, to be stressed and overthink everything? If you have, then you already have some awareness of the concept of Parts.

Sometimes we use different phrases and sentences, such as:

- A bit of me feels this way and a bit of me feels that way'.
- Or 'on one hand, I want this, on the other hand, I want that'.

In all of these examples, we can sense an inner conflict, where we are being pulled in different and contradictory directions.

Often, we notice these Parts at work, but almost seem powerless to stop them. You can see this in someone who is dûing drinking too much as they feel the pull between:

- Being clear they need to stop drinking on one hand.
- And on the other hand, reaching for that bottle of wine.

Or someone who has committed to shifting some weight and:

- Wants to stick to their plan of eating healthily and exercising.
- And, yet, they find themselves in the aisle of a supermarket gazing longingly at a chocolate cake.

In some of the earlier IWT steps, Parts showed up, for example in IWT 11, 'Letting go of blame', where the notes mentioned that sometimes 'you may find some sense of resistance, objection or reluctance to letting it go'. This is another common way of describing the presence of inner conflict and Parts. These kinds of conflicts are so common that some great innovators in therapy have created approaches for addressing and resolving them. Much of the work I'll be describing here is built on their original ideas, so, if you want to discover more about their work, I'd suggest checking out Fritz Perls, Virginia Satir and

Connirae Andreas[37-39].

Good Or Bad Parts?

You may have also noticed that trying to fight your way through these kinds of inner conflicts takes up so much energy. It's a little like going to the supermarket and finding you have picked a trolley that has three perfectly good wheels and one that seems to have a mind of its own. If you've had this experience, you'll know how much extra force is required to get that trolley moving in a straight direction, just because of that one contrary wheel.

When we come across inner conflicts, we often feel that one Part is good and the other one is less good, or bad. In the 'drinking too much' example the Part that wants us to stop drinking will probably be considered to be the good one and the one that wants to continue drinking is likely labelled as the bad Part. Certain solutions naturally follow from this kind of good/bad thinking. We will often attempt to force our way through the conflict, trying:

- To focus on the 'good' Part.
- And get rid of the 'bad' one.

We attempt to shut that 'bad' Part up or move it far away, ignore it, sedate or medicate it, starve it or pretend it's not there, and so on. This takes a lot of energy to do, doesn't resolve the issue, and creates a further problem. If, for example, we choose to ignore that cake in the supermarket, we will probably spend some time dûing regretful thinking about how great that cake would be if only we'd bought and eaten it. These thoughts are driven by that Part of us that wanted a cake because it's annoyed and frustrated it hasn't got what it wanted.

However, if we buy and eat that cake, we may spend the rest of the day dûing feeling remorseful for breaking our commitment to eating healthily. This is driven by the Part that wanted us to stick to our plan. Notice how we're still trapped by this conflict as whichever option we choose doesn't result in joy or peace, all we've done is further increased that sense of tension and conflict within us.

Another Way

As this approach doesn't seem to produce great results, other ways of thinking about this conflict can be incredibly useful here. Imagine two neighbours have been in conflict for some time and Jo has the job of finding a peaceful and mutually agreeable solution that resolves their issues. A meeting is arranged with both neighbours attending, where Jo will take the role of mediator. As they arrive Jo says to neighbour 1, 'I completely understand how difficult it has been for you and I know that you have right on your side. I am going to work to make sure you get what you want.' Jo turns to neighbour 2 and says, 'I can hardly believe you have the nerve to show your face here, you are nothing but trouble and have unreasonably caused all this conflict'. You can imagine what will happen next. Neighbour 2, who sees that Jo has already decided to take the side of neighbour 1 now knows they will not get a fair hearing. They know there is no point in staying and will leave the meeting and the conflict will continue. This is because Jo was supposed to take on the role of a mediator and needed to be able to listen with an open mind, giving everyone a fair hearing and not taking sides. Instead, Jo has been biased against neighbour 2 and partisan and prejudicial in favouring neighbour 1. It is obvious that Jo's approach here is not useful and will inflame the situation rather than resolve it.

But, when we think about it, this is exactly how we have been trying to resolve our inner conflicts, judging one as good or bad, favouring one and trying to punish the other. So, it's no surprise that that hasn't worked well either. What we need is a new perspective, one in which we can be open to see the Parts in a new light, where we can genuinely listen to them and understand them. But that is a big ask, as these Parts have often caused us all sorts of trouble over the years (for example the Part that's made us drink too much, have arguments or behave like a sulky child) so there are several steps we'll cover that will help us achieve this Transformational shift. I'll cover the ideas first so you're familiar with them. This will make it much simpler to apply them as they show up in the various stages of the Parts IWT 17.

Parts As A Mini-You

In the previous section, I referred to these Parts almost as if they are independently acting aspects within us. You can see this with the phrase 'these thoughts were driven by that Part that wanted the cake and it's annoyed'. This is quite a useful way to think about Parts, although they're quite different from the mental health issues of having multiple or sub-personalities. It's viewing them as though they are small versions or elements of us working toward a particular set of agendas. Each Part will need your focused care and attention, almost as if it is a mini version of you that needs your help support and guidance. Having this in mind will help as we move through the process. It will help us understand why these Parts exist and what we need to do to resolve this inner conflict. But before we go into that, just pause for a moment and think about where you find yourself dûing conflict with yourself, where you dû those inner arguments or where your unconscious mind or your body seems to be dûing working against you and your goals. Imagine what would it be like to not have to use up that energy anymore in that fight. What would it be like if you could stop draining yourself with those conflicts and instead have all that energy available for you to achieve what you wanted in your life?

LEARNING TO LOVE YOUR PARTS

We've now realised that being hard on these Parts is probably not going to move us forward, so we're going to need to bring Kindness to the Parts IWT 17. This section provides the reasons why it's appropriate, as well as necessary, to be kind to these Parts of ourselves. Even though they often appear to be working toward very different agendas than the ones we want. We can see this difference in the example we'll use in the sections below of 'a Part that wants peacefulness and acceptance' (probably labelled as the 'good' Part) and 'a Part that wants us to stay upset and angry' (probably labelled as the 'bad' Part). It's worth noting here that I'm going to stop using the phrases the 'good' and 'bad' Parts at this point, as we need to move away from thinking of those Parts in terms of those conflict-supporting labels. To shift from this stuck conflict into something transformational and life-affirming we will need to take on a number of unfamiliar ways of thinking about Parts. So, put your 'growth' hat on and, connecting deeply to the Gateway State of Curiosity, let's go...

1 We Were Younger

The first reason for being kind to these Parts is found by considering where these issues and behaviours come from. The origin of why we, or our Parts, dû what we dû can be found in our past and the decisions we made about how to deal with the world when we were younger. Those decisions were naturally limited due to our age and inexperience where:

a) We had less understanding of the world than we do now. As children, we may have found many things 'upsetting' that now we would view in a very different way. This is true of being a young child, but equally applies to us as teenagers (although we may have thought we knew all about the world by then), and to us in our 20s or even in our more recent past.

b) We were probably learning our behaviours from what we observed our parents, adults, and peers around us doing. These people, and their MAPPS, may not have been the best reference points for picking our future behavioural choices. Consider how little instruction and life experience most new parents have in the complex skills of child-rearing. If this resulted in, for example, a child being shown 'irritation as a way of dealing with life's problems', they could easily take on those anger-based behaviours, independent of how successful those strategies were.

c) We had a much smaller range of behaviours to choose from because of our age. A 5-year-old doesn't tend to have the same skill set to manage complex relationships or difficult emotions as a 40-year-old with life experience - although you've probably met some 40-year-olds whose behaviour

seems to be driven by their 5-year-old experiences...
Dûing upset as a child may produce a very helpful
response from adults around us who may rush to
take care of us. This 'upset' response may become
less useful, or successful, over time.

d) Due to our age, not all the choices we may have
wanted were available to us. When we're younger
our options are limited by the environment we are in
at that time, so dûing upset may have been one of
the only options available to us to get some help or
support we needed at the time. Examples of lack of
choice include having to attend a school that didn't
suit us, not being able to swap teachers even if they
were a poor fit for us, unavoidable school bullies,
having to follow adults' instructions, not being able
to move out of a toxic family/friendship group as we
were only 8 years old, etc.

Given all this, maybe we need to be kinder to ourselves for the fact that
these behaviours were generated at a very different time in our lives
and in very different situations.

2 Why These Behaviours Were Built

The second reason for bringing Kindness to these Parts comes from
understanding why they were created. Their development can be traced
through the following set of steps:

a) We came across something new and unexpected.
Maybe it was someone's difficult or surprising
behaviour or a deeply unfamiliar situation. We didn't
understand it and didn't know what to do, which left
us feeling confused and paralysed due to having no
MAPP or plan of action to follow for this kind of
situation. We realised we needed to make some
sense of what was happening so we could make a
plan to deal with it. This attempt to understand and
deal with it was our best guess. It may not have been
that accurate, as it was based on our more youthful

version of how the world works (as described in the section above), but it helped more than having no idea what was going on. This new incomplete understanding creates a **new belief**, or guess, of how the world is. This guess, although incomplete and inaccurate, is useful because it helps us work out **what to do to** resolve the situation. In the 'upset and angry' example above: We faced a new and surprising situation and we worked out: We didn't understand it, that this kind of thing was too much for us to deal with, and we needed help (this is the new belief). We responded by dûing upset. Someone came to help us. We felt a bit better as a result. Therefore, dûing upset seems to work as a solution to this type of problem (the new behaviour).

b) And it's good enough because, in this case, we got through the situation and survived. We recognised this belief and behaviour had helped us do that. Later, when other similar situations occurred, we discovered this new way of thinking and behaving helped there too. Each time it worked we felt more certain that our understanding of the world was correct, and that our responses were the best way of dealing with these kinds of things. As a result, the belief started to become, through experience, a reliable fact, and the behaviour we'd built as a response, seemed like the correct response. In the example, each time we responded with 'upset' we got assistance that made things better. This confirmed to us that 'dûing upset' is a useful response to many situations.

c) We used it so often that, rather than seeing it as a useful guide for dealing with those kinds of situations, when we were young, we mistook this MAPP for the truth. In the example, we dû 'upset' as a response to those kinds of situations, but now it no longer works. No one comes to our aid, and we're left feeling that we've not got the skills of 'being calm' that others seem to have to deal with these kinds of everyday events.

Applying 1 and 2
It can be helpful to summarise these first two steps in a simpler overview.

- This behaviour has its origins in an earlier, confusing time in our life.
- It was our younger self's best attempt to find an effective temporary solution.
- The solution worked quite well for us initially.
- And continued to work well on many subsequent occasions.

As we recognise this, it becomes easier to see these old behaviours in a kinder light. Let's apply it to a different example, that of wanting to 'do calm' but 'dûing stress' instead.

Here we have a Part of us that responds by dûing stress to new situations and instead of thinking of this as the 'bad' it might be better to call it the 'young' Part. We know it's not helpful when we go to interviews or parties where we don't know many people. We want to be calm and relaxed, as we know that will help us more but we keep falling into dûing stress instead.

But notice what happens when we apply our new thinking to the 'young' Part. Let's imagine we discover it's been hard at work for us since we were 5. Seeing it through the mindset of a five-year-old get a sense of what it might be like to deal with a surprising and maybe unpleasant situation, like meeting new people.

1. We Were Younger
   a. **We had less understanding of the world than we do now**. As a young child of 5, the world is indeed likely to look much scarier to us than to a worldly-wise

adult. Meeting a new group of school kids, or strangers at a party could be quite challenging to our young and unprepared nervous system. Also bear in mind that when we're young and vulnerable, our body is hardwired to look for difficulty and danger as a safety mechanism.

b. **We were probably learning our behaviours from what we observed our parents, adults, and peers around us doing.** How did the responsible adults around us behave? Were they dûing calm or stressed much of the time? Were they insightful and skilled at helping us deal with these new situations? Or did they just throw us in and expect us to get on with it?

c. **We had a much smaller range of behaviours to choose from because of our age.** Had anyone taught us the skills we needed to stay calm in these situations? Did we have evidence that if we dîd stressed and scared that people ran to our rescue? Did we have the range of skills we have now?

d. **Our options were limited by the environment we were in at that time.** Were we forced to do things we didn't want to? Was this one way of making sure people knew we weren't happy with the situation?

2. Why These Behaviours Were Built

a. **We came across something new and unexpected.** As adults, we are so used to understanding the world that getting in touch with the sense of something being completely WEIRD and NEW is very unfamiliar and takes a bit of work to connect with. We have to think of some extremely weird things to get a sense of this so, maybe imagine something that is so out of your normal experience, like waking up to an alien invasion, or finding yourself in someone else's body, something you have no MAPP for. Now, these options don't quite fully give us the sense of having no idea what's going on - because we'd say 'oh it's an alien invasion/body swap situation like I've seen in the movies' - but for the five-year-old, this 'new people' situation is COMPLETELY uncharted territory. When you have a bit of a sense of this, you can imagine how they would need to create the best understanding they could of it this weirdness and from that create a plan of action for how to survive it.

b. **And it's good enough because we got through the situation and survived.** Imagine the strategy you designed worked this time - maybe people took care of you because you were upset, maybe you were quiet so no one asked you any questions, maybe you clung to your mum's leg and wouldn't let go, maybe you escaped to the safety of the garden - and it worked well in many other instances. As a result, you used this response every time. And for many years it worked brilliantly.

With all this going on in such a young child's life, maybe we can see that they did a great job of trying to manage the crazy situation they found themselves thrown into, and instead of being hard on this Part, we should be seeing it in a new, kinder, and more appreciative light?

3 We Always Do Our Best and Positive Intentions

This information about how limited our problem-solving was at that younger age guides us to the third reason for being nice to these Parts. It's the recognition that, throughout our lives, independent of how great or appalling our choices, decisions and behaviours have turned out to be, each one of them was our best attempt at that time. We didn't go out of our way to create a bad choice or design a self-destructive behaviour or habit to cause ourselves trouble. It was just our best and probably the only option to get through that situation based on what we knew at that time. Keep this important idea in mind: every solution, behaviour and understanding we came up with was driven by the positive goal of finding a way to get through that situation, so we could survive, move on and have a chance to have a better life. This underlying drive, called a Positive Intention (PI), can be identified in any behaviour, no matter how damaging it appears to be, as can be seen in these examples:

Gambling

Consider a gambler who throws even more money chasing a loss. He is trying the only strategy he knows to try and recoup his debts and come out winning. He hopes one more throw of the dice will result in a big win, resolving his problems, and allow him to get back on track to his PI, a better life.

The issue here is whether that tried and trusted behaviour that worked in the past is still useful in this new situation. As most of us know, for the majority of gamblers the answer is 'No, it's not'.

Angry Outbursts

As a child, it's reasonable to shout, scream and sometimes lash out when we're not getting what we want or when we need help or attention. However, later in life, if we find ourselves using this same strategy when we need help, it may not be as effective and may have some severe side effects, destroying relationships, getting us in trouble with the authorities etc. We can identify that the PI of the behaviour, to get us assistance, which will help us find our way through the situation better, and move towards a better life, is a valuable goal. It's just that those behaviours don't work that well in the adult world we now live in.

Harmful Drug Use

Harmful drug use is destructive to our health, relationships, happiness, quality of life and so much more[1]. However, there's a range of research identifying the PIs that drive people to use very dangerous and life-destroying drugs are often an attempt to achieve good things in their lives[40]. It's their previously effective method of dealing with stress, sedating themselves from anxiety or reality, and one way to get a sense, however fleeting, of joy. Interestingly this example suggests how long

Parts have been around in human history, as over 5000 years ago that the word *Hul* was used by the Sumerians to mean both Opium and Joy.

Paradoxes

From these examples, we can observe one of the most curious findings of working with Parts. Much of the time:

- The 'problem' behaviour, such as taking drugs, which increases stress and reduces our quality of life,
- Achieves completely the opposite of the original purpose of that behaviour, in this case, joy and less stress

Years ago, I saw someone in their late 30s who had been a smoker since their teens and wanted to stop. But every time she did stop, a strange thing happened, she became (dîd) ill. And every time she started smoking again her illness went away (she stopped dûing it). The use of dû here may sound strange as it refers to illness, but you may remember how useful it was to use dû with pain and inflammation, and, as you read on you'll discover why it's the most accurate description of what was going in in her health...

We identified there was:

1. One Part wanting her to stop smoking
2. And another one that appeared to want to continue. This second Part was the one that seemed to make her ill every time she stopped smoking and restored her health every time she started again.

As we explored this from a Parts perspective some interesting information surfaced. When she was young her parents frequently moved and each time she started at a new school. As can often happen, being the 'New Girl' meant she had a tough time fitting in. As a result, she dîd hating school and had/dîd much illness, especially stomach aches and pains, some of which she feigned, as being ill meant she got to stay at home. When her long-term unexplained stomach symptoms required exploratory surgery, she was one of the happiest children you'd ever see going into the operating theatre, as she knew this meant she would have at least a few weeks away from school. This identifies just how difficult school life was for her. We can see the PI of being ill here is to avoid school, reduce stress and, hopefully, have a better life.

One day, at school, she was wandering around and stumbled into the area where the 'naughty' kids who smoked hung out. They encouraged her to try a cigarette, which she lit, but unfortunately for her, it was just at that moment that the head teacher appeared. All the other kids knew the drill and ran away as quickly as they could, leaving her all alone, standing in front of the head teacher, holding a smouldering cigarette.

The head teacher looked at her sternly and told her he would deal with her at the next morning's assembly. The next morning, as the whole school gathered in the hall, the head teacher called her up on stage and told everyone what a bad example she had set by smoking on the school premises.

However, being told off in this way had unexpected side effects. Instead, as the headteacher had hoped of warning the children off smoking, it transformed her, in their eyes, into the rebellious, cool kid. Someone so dangerous and exciting that she needed to be personally told off in front of everyone by the head teacher himself. As a result, everyone wanted to know her, and she started having more friends than she could ever imagine. And the more she smoked, the more her reputation as a sophisticated rebel grew. As she started to enjoy going to school and hanging out with her new friends, there was no longer a reason to be ill enough to miss school.

Smoking, it turned out, was an effective behaviour for keeping her well and stopped her from being ill.

As she moved schools, and later when starting new jobs or going out socially, the same behaviour worked each time and she found it easy to rapidly make friends with the other smokers.

Years later, when she wanted to stop smoking, that Part that was created, at that young age, in those very specific circumstances, launched into action.

When she 'dangerously' (from its world MAPP) stopped smoking (as it knew smoking was essential for her health) it made her ill, just as it had been built to do. When she started smoking again (back on the path to health, danger averted) it restored her health and made her well.

You cannot fault the logic of this Part, based on those original experiences. It was doing exactly what it was supposed to do. But, of course, we can also see the paradox here, as we know that smoking does not make you well and significantly damages your health. So:

- The behaviour (smoking)
- Is achieving the opposite of what it was originally intended to do (keep her healthy).

Because of these paradoxes, the PI may not initially be obvious from observing the 'difficult' behaviour. It can take a little time and some different ways of thinking to uncover these. In the Parts IWT 17 you'll learn how to discover a Part's hidden PI, using some clever but simple questions. However, before you can have a chance to discover its PI you'll need to gain its trust and take the role of the kind and supportive mediator that we've been exploring in detail in these steps. A conflict resolution would be doomed if the mediator viewed someone as 'annoying, difficult or bad'. They have to build trust with everyone involved first. So how do we do this with Parts when our experience is often that they have been difficult to live with?

4 Why Are Parts So Persistent And Noisy

The fourth reason for shifting our relationship to these Parts comes from understanding why they are so noisy - they're certainly great at getting your attention - and why they are so persistent and resilient. Maybe you've noticed that when we apply those old strategies of trying to banish, destroy or sedate them, and we think we've achieved it, they seem to bounce back.

This is because these Parts were built for an important purpose, their PI, as a solution to a challenging problem, and this PI is still super important. From the examples above, the 'keep smoking' Part wanted to keep that client 'healthy and well', the 'drug using' Part wanted joy, the 'stress' and 'angry' Parts wanted help so they could find solutions, the 'gambling' Part wanted a better life. Those are all great things and such important missions that those Parts are just not prepared to give up on you having those PIs. And you wouldn't want to lose these PIs from your life either. This is why they are so persistent and resilient.

Thankfully, each Part is absolutely committed to delivering its PI, so when you're out of step with that, it will make sure you hear it, by getting your attention in some unmissable way. And that's why it's noisy.

Car designers use the same strategy. If you are driving at speed down a motorway and a flashing red light appears in the middle of the dashboard, you stop to see what that light means and how to fix it. It's signalling important information that may save your life or the life of your car, so it's designed to be annoying and to get your attention. Being cross with it because it's interfering with your peaceful journey or sticking some tape over it so you can't see it is probably not the best way to deal with this. We easily separate the action 'flashing red light = annoying', from the PI 'informing me to keep me safe'.

Wake-up alarms are the same, if they were quiet and unobtrusive, they'd fail at doing their job.

From this, we can recognise how these Parts are incredibly well designed based on those specific experiences you had when you were younger. When you consider it, they have some extraordinary skills and qualities:

- They are **committed** to finding ways to get something incredibly important for you - their PI.
- They have the inbuilt ability to be incredibly **resilient and persistent**. When it's been told to go away, for just doing

what you instructed it to do, it brushes off your dismissal, resiliently bouncing back, coming back as strong as before.

- They are amazing at **alerting** you when you are going off track from delivering on that vital positive intention. They are experts at getting your attention.
- They are also incredibly **creative**, coming up with multiple ways to deliver on their mission, or if you're not listening to them, creating new, increasingly 'noisy' ways to get your attention.
- They're incredibly **reliable**, and despite an absence of maintenance, it never takes a day off sick or needs a holiday.

These qualities, in bold, which this Part has been continually demonstrating are quite extraordinary ones and something that many of us want more access to. What if we could have this Part working with us, providing these qualities where we most need them in our life? This realisation helps us to see the value in this Part even more. We can recognise that its design is second to none. It's like a car that starts when it's cold, raining or baking hot and never breaks down. It's the car you would never sell because it's so reliable.

The only problem is that this Part is resiliently trying to get that all-important PI for us using the limited set of skills and the underdeveloped MAPP it had available when we were younger.

Those skills worked well for years, but as time moved on and new more complex situations arose, they became less and less effective. This Part is stuck in time, still seeing the world as we understood it when we designed it. Information about new skills, new learnings, and new MAPP updates rarely get to that Part, so it has never discovered that the world has changed. As a result, it carries on trying to fix problems using the understanding it had of the world when we first came across this issue as a youngster. Never quitting, never complaining, always working.

And yet, in recent years, every time this Part turns up, we've given it a hard time being annoyed and frustrated with it, wishing it would just go away. This reasonable response is because we only experience the Part from its annoying 'persistent and noisy' behaviours rather than getting in touch with its powerful PI. A vital part of transforming your relationship to the Part is to see it in this new light and to begin to value its rarely recognised but incredible skills and qualities.

SUMMARY OF REASONS FOR BEING KIND TO PARTS
We've covered a lot of ground here in our exploration of Parts and why we need to see them in a different kinder light. This important first step often involves regaining its trust. This is because, as far as it's concerned, we've treated it pretty badly over the years, when all it's been doing is working hard for us, in exactly the way we asked it to do all those years ago. It might even be a little wary of us because of the way it's been treated. Luckily, with this new knowledge about Parts and the steps of the Parts IWT 17 we will, with some care, be able to forge a new trusting relationship with it.

You may have found that just by engaging in these ideas things have already started to shift, and you may have experienced some 'Aha, so that's why I dû that!' moments already.

From this exploration you should now recognise:

- That continuing to struggle against Parts of ourselves hasn't worked that well and maybe it's time for a new less conflictual approach.
- That 'problem' behaviour has a good reason for existing - it was created by a younger you that was dealing with a difficult situation.
- The choices that the younger you made were based on the information you had available at that time about who you were and what was possible.
- That every decision you made was the best and probably only choice that you could have made at that time to deal with a challenging situation.

- That being the case, you can let yourself off the hook for dûing some of these things and be kind to yourself whilst you help these Parts get updated.
- That no Part is good or bad, but they may have got stuck in time.
- That you need to take the role of a kind mediator.
- That these Parts have incredibly valuable qualities.
- That you can separate the 'unhelpful' behaviours you dû, such as having an argument, gambling, or using substances from the reason that you're dûing them (the PI).
- Often the Part's behaviour (e.g., smoking) is the opposite of its PI (e.g., to be well).
- That you might need to be much nicer to these Parts than you've ever been to finally resolve this inner struggle.

Now that we've done this important groundwork, we can use our growing IW skills to discover how to resolve the conflict, using the Parts IWT 17. So, get ready for something quite special, as many find this process produces insight, pleasant feelings of emotional release and quite extraordinary and life-enhancing transformations.

IWT 17: Parts

Get prepared as before. Make sure there is about 1 metre of space to the left, the right and in front of you.

Take one Part that you notice has been showing up and causing issues for you and have this as the focus for this IWT (for information on the signs that Parts are present see the notes after the IWT). Stand in the 'You' position and take 5 deep, easy breaths.

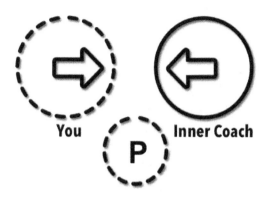

1. Reconnect with the Gateway States of 'Self-Kindness' and 'Transformation' you accessed in IWT 4 and 15.
2. Step into this powerful and important Part (marked by P on the map) and connect with any of the familiar feelings or phrases this Part gives you when you feel its presence. Many will notice it has colour, temperature, size, and if it's hard or soft, etc.
3. Now step into the Inner Coach and speak directly to that Part. Take the role of the mediator by acknowledging this Part and being kind to it using the background work we've covered, knowing:
   a. You created it in response to a difficult situation.
   b. At that time this was the best and probably the only sensible and appropriate response.
   c. Ever since it's just been doing its job, just as you asked it to.
   d. It has some amazing qualities that you might like to have more of in your life.

   Let it know you just want to listen and understand what it has to say.

4. Step over into P and notice how, by being nice to it in this way, it changes how it feels. You should feel emotional or

a sense of relief; that it's not the enemy anymore; or a softening or reduction in size, temperature or colour. If there's no change, go back and genuinely reassure it that you deeply appreciate it for how hard it has been working for you, until you sense a shift.

5. Step back to the Inner Coach. Knowing that Part is great at communicating to get your attention, it now has a chance to finally be heard by you in a new way. Say to that Part:

    a. 'I'm going to ask you a question and the answer will be a number. The question is how old were you when you created this behaviour?' Step to P and answer*.

    b. Step back to the Inner Coach, see it as 'you at that age' and thank it again (as in step 3) as you would someone who was that young. Step to P and notice how that further changes how it feels.

6. Now we've made friends with it, we can discover its PI. Step into the Inner Coach ask, 'What is it that you want **for** me that's positive, through doing this behaviour?'

7. Step into P and respond.

8. Step back to the Inner Coach and thank it for its answer. Keep on asking, 'What is it that you want **for** me that's even more positive than that?' and answering and thanking, stepping from Inner Coach to P each time, until you get a PI that is deeply positive *.

---

9. You may have already noticed that this Part was part of a greater whole, which got separated a long time ago.

    a. As the Inner Coach ask 'You', 'As you now recognise the Part is fully committed to this positive purpose (it's PI) would it be ok to welcome back this updated Part of you as it works in new ways towards its important PI?'

    b. Step into 'You' and find your answer. If it is 'yes', reach over to that old Part in P and hug it and let it flow into 'You'. Let it merge and re-join with you, longer works. No one comes to our aid, and we're left feeling that we've not got the skills of 'being calm' that others seem to have to deal with these kinds of everyday events.

Applying 1 and 2

It can be helpful to summarise these first two steps in a simpler overview.

- This behaviour has its origins in an earlier, confusing time in our life.
- It was our younger self's best attempt to find an effective temporary solution.
- The solution worked quite well for us initially.
- And continued to work well on many subsequent occasions.

As we recognise this, it becomes easier to see these old behaviours in a kinder light. Let's apply it to a different example, that of wanting to 'do calm' but 'dûing stress' instead.

Here we have a Part of us that responds by dûing stress to new situations and instead of thinking of this as the 'bad' it might be better to call it the 'young' Part. We know it's not helpful when we go to interviews or parties where we don't know many people. We want to be calm and relaxed, as we know that will help us more but we keep falling into dûing stress instead.

But notice what happens when we apply our new thinking to the 'young' Part. Let's imagine we discover it's been hard at work for us since we were 5. Seeing it through the mindset of a five-year-old get a sense of what it might be like to deal with a surprising and maybe unpleasant situation, like meeting new people.

1. We Were Younger
   a. **We had less understanding of the world than we do now.** As a young child of 5, the world is indeed likely to look much scarier to us than to a worldly-wise

version of how the world works (as described in the section above), but it helped more than having no idea what was going on. This new incomplete understanding creates a **new belief**, or guess, of how the world is. This guess, although incomplete and inaccurate, is useful because it helps us work out **what to do to** resolve the situation. In the 'upset and angry' example above: We faced a new and surprising situation and we worked out: We didn't understand it, that this kind of thing was too much for us to deal with, and we needed help (this is the new belief). We responded by dûing upset. Someone came to help us. We felt a bit better as a result. Therefore, dûing upset seems to work as a solution to this type of problem (the new behaviour).

b) And it's good enough because, in this case, we got through the situation and survived. We recognised this belief and behaviour had helped us do that. Later, when other similar situations occurred, we discovered this new way of thinking and behaving helped there too. Each time it worked we felt more certain that our understanding of the world was correct, and that our responses were the best way of dealing with these kinds of things. As a result, the belief started to become, through experience, a reliable fact, and the behaviour we'd built as a response, seemed like the correct response. In the example, each time we responded with 'upset' we got assistance that made things better. This confirmed to us that 'dûing upset' is a useful response to many situations.

c) We used it so often that, rather than seeing it as a useful guide for dealing with those kinds of situations, when we were young, we mistook this MAPP for the truth. In the example, we dû 'upset' as a response to those kinds of situations, but now it no forming a new greater whole which includes all that was of value in it and letting go of anything outdated or no longer serves your shared PI. Often, you will experience some interesting feelings throughout your body as this integration happens.

c. If there is any sense of 'objection' to this new arrangement, consider that 'objection' to be another Part. Place it in a space next to the original P and take it through the same process.

---

10. In a moment this more complete You and your Inner Coach are going to step together in, and through, that 'Space' that represents the situation in the past where you used to dû that old behaviour. Feeling this new more complete sense of yourself, turn towards the 'Space' and step in, and through it. Hear, see, imagine, and feel the presence and support of your Inner Coach walking next to You. Notice how it feels to move in this new way through this area of your life that used to dû stuck.

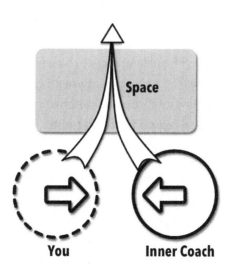

11. Step beyond it, to the head of the arrow, with your Inner Coach beside You, and look back. How does it feel to see and experience this change?

12. Staying here, reconnect with the Gateway State of Kindness again and feel it flowing through you and anyone else involved. Flowing through those old places where you used to dû stuck, in a completely new way, with this new sense of who you are. Notice how you feel differently now. How does having this transform your experience of the world? What does it feel like to have this new behaviour, powered by that brilliantly effective old neurology, automatically show up each time you need it?

In this process, you have done some very important and powerful change work, so take a little bit of time to learn these new understandings and new arrangements within you to settle and integrate. You may want to go for a walk in nature just to help with this process.

*Notes:
Signs of Parts: There are many ways that Parts can show up in your life. These include self-sabotaging behaviours or ways of thinking, dissipated energy, blocks, and stuckness, unreasonably reactive responses to situations or others (anger, sulking, etc.), behaving like a child/teenager (when you're not anymore), pointless arguments, confusion, unfulfilled intentions, limiting beliefs, and some symptoms, especially those that seem to have no medical reason for being there.

Step 5: The number may or may not be the one you expect, just allow the Part to reply with the number it feels is appropriate. Quite often the number is younger than ten years old, with 5 being common, but go with whatever number it gives you. Sometimes it can feel like you're guessing or making up a number, but this is fine, it's a sign that you're doing something a little unfamiliar and tapping into your unconscious, which is where this Part operates from. After working in this way for over three decades, I've found that, as there are so many possible ages to choose from, there is always a good reason for this period of your life being identified as important in the development of the Part. Spend a little time thinking about that period of your life, what was going on then, and how this connects with what this Part has been doing in your life since then.

Step 6: Sometimes people misread this and ask, 'What do you want **FROM** me?' This question suggests the Part is trying to get them to do something for it, when in fact, it's the opposite - this Part is trying to be of service to them in some way - it's working **FOR** them.
There are also a few different ways of asking for a PI, so try these variations out and see what works best for you:

- What have you always wanted for me that's positive?
- What have you been trying to get for me all this time?
- What did you originally want for me?

Step 8: Is it a PI yet? - Sometimes the Part's first answers to 'What is it that you want that's positive for me through doing this behaviour?' can result in an answer that is negative, such as 'to make you feel bad' or 'to make you stressed'.

Other times the answer will sound positive but actually be a hidden negative, which we first discussed in Chapter 3. Common examples are:

- To be safe.
- To feel secure and protected.
- Free from.

These are good examples of 'away from' statements; safe *from* what? Even 'freedom' is usually an 'away from' as it often means to be free *from* something. As a result, these answers are a reminder to find a deeper and more authentically positive intention. When you have found its true PI, it will make the 'merging together' steps of the process simple and easy, as it will be such an obviously great choice to have this 'Part' of us back on the team and fully integrated with us.

To convert one of these negative or hidden negatives into a PI ask, **'And if you had that what would it give you that's positive?'**

SUMMARY OF PARTS IWT

Since I first came across the extraordinary power of working with Parts in the 1990s, I've seen people use these ideas to change such a huge range of issues. These include strong persistent symptoms, such as food intolerances, IBS, and pain; skin issues, rashes, and eczema; immune system issues such as asthma and ulcerative colitis; emotional and psychological issues, including anger, self-doubt, and eating disorders; damaging habits and addictions, and a range of other issues that had blighted peoples' lives for decades.

There are three core principles that underlie this approach. First, being deeply compassionate and kind to these Parts of us that have been working for us for so long; second, rediscovering their positive intention; third, which allows the Parts to see their shared purpose, integrate and resolve the conflict. Following these integrative and Kindness based steps has been life-changing for so many people. You can see from the exploration that there is a nuanced skill set required to work with this fascinating approach. This means that occasionally we might realise we need some expert support to guide us through this process, providing insight that helps unlock our way forward. Remember wisdom doesn't mean doing it all by yourself, it means knowing when help might be useful. Although in most cases you'll find, as so many others have, that this IWT version of working with Parts is a simple way to tap into new levels of Self-Kindness and Transformation.

'Every Behaviour Is Driven By The Positive Goal Of Finding A Way To Get Through That Situation.'

CHAPTER 20: CONNECTION

LEVELS OF CONNECTION
We have all experienced the Gateway State of Connection, as it shows up in everyday situations when we sense that bond with friends and loved ones, or simply say 'Hi' to people in the street. We'll be looking at this human level of Connection, and what happens when we dû disconnected or at odds with others, and how we can apply IW to these situations.

Connection can also be experienced at a much deeper level, where we sense the connection between us and the much bigger systems we're part of. Examples of this type of connection include times when we refocus on the fact that we're part of the human species, nature, the global ecosystem, the solar system, or even the vastness of space.

We're going to focus on all these aspects of Connection in a range of IWTs to make change. But let's start by exploring some ways to get a sense of this Gateway State of connection.

IWT 18: Connection
Sit down quietly in a space where you won't be disturbed, take 5 deep breaths, and connect with the Gateway State of Curiosity that we connected with in IWT 5. Read each section through first, and then, using your imagination, take yourself on the journey suggested at the end of each section.

AIR
Consider that the air that you're breathing in is part of the planet's atmosphere that circulates around the entire globe. In your breath, there are some Oxygen molecules (O_2). O here is the symbol for an Oxygen atom and the $_2$ denotes that they love to travel in pairs, as even atoms love to be Connected. The O_2 in the air you're breathing in was produced by plants or plankton (tiny lifeforms) in the seas, somewhere on the planet. They created it by drawing in the Carbon Dioxide (CO_2) breathed out by us and all the other animals and using sunlight to

convert that into Oxygen (O_2) and Carbon (C). This Carbon will be used by the plants to create sugars and complex molecules, which will form the building blocks of the food we eat, which we will use to power and repair our bodies.

AIR JOURNEY

1. Imagine riding on a stream of Oxygen molecules (O_2) that are in the air you're breathing in right now. Follow them on their journey as they are carried around your body to wherever they are needed.
2. Then follow them as they are used and then combined with Carbon atoms (C) and breathed out as Carbon Dioxide molecules (CO_2) to flow through the air, travelling around the world, visiting any number of fascinating destinations.
3. Follow the CO_2 molecules until they are taken in again by plants or other creatures to be part of their world for a while. Eventually, the CO_2 molecules will once again be separated into Oxygen (O_2) and Carbon (C) by the plants.
4. Follow these Oxygen molecules (O_2) on their journey back to being breathed in by you again. Cycle back to step 1. This is the cyclical journey these atoms and molecules have endlessly been part of for hundreds of thousands of years.

WATER

The water currently in our body is only temporarily there. It flows in a constant cycle, as we, and other living things, take it in as water from rain, snow, rivers, and lakes and as part of the food we eat. We use it as a vital element in so many body processes and then send it back into the soil, air, rivers, lakes, and oceans. From there, it returns to us again as rain, snow, rivers, and lakes as the cycle repeats. Follow the journey below.

WATER JOURNEY

1. Imagine being a drop of water drifting down as rain through a deep green forest. It rests on the leaves before finding its way down to the forest floor. There it just soaks

through the soil, joining with other raindrops and forming the beginnings of a tiny, underground stream. Eventually, it bubbles out of the soil as a spring and flows away from the forest.

2. Sometimes it flows slowly, sometimes finding its way around boulders, through tree roots, and tangles, but always on towards the sea. Sometimes it lingers long, meandering through a sun-soaked meadow. Other times, it flows into a deep still lake. It rests there as time passes before eventually, flowing onward towards the sea. Sometimes it flows through towns, cities, valleys, and wide open plains. Drenched by the sun, covered in a canopy of blue sky. But always, towards the sea. And eventually, it reaches what we may think is its journey's end. The estuary, where the river meets the sea. And there it transforms from fresh water to salty seawater.

3. It becomes part of the vast ocean, and it's carried on the currents, sometimes North, West, South or East. Sometimes the water's cooler, other times it's warmer. Sometimes it's so warm that it rises as mist, higher and higher, into the atmosphere. Finally, it forms fluffy clouds that drift, carried on the currents of the wind.

4. Sometimes the precious cargo of rain falls from the clouds as it crosses a barren desert. Here, it looks as if nothing could ever grow there, but the rain falls, and within hours and days, the desert transforms into a carpet of beautiful hues, of purples, pinks, yellows, and blues. Sometimes it falls over a lake, or an ocean, or as snow on a high mountainside.

5. Sometimes it falls over fertile fields, irrigating the crops to help them grow so they can be harvested to feed you. When you eat them, that water temporarily becomes part of you, hydrating you and playing a pivotal role in so many vital processes in your body, before being released and returning back to this cycle.

6. Sometimes it falls over a deep green forest. Drifting down as rain, it rests on the leaves before finding its way down to the forest floor. There it just soaks through the soil, joining with other raindrops and forming the beginnings of a tiny, underground stream. Eventually, it bubbles out of the soil as a spring and flows away from the forest. Sometimes it flows slowly, sometimes finding its way around boulders, through tree roots, and tangles, but always on towards the sea.

EARTH

As the earth's crust is continuous across the planet's surface, and there are no unattached sections, the ground we're on right now connects to all other parts of the world. So, wherever you are right now in the world, that section of the earth beneath you, and you, are in touch with every other piece of earth on the planet.

EARTH JOURNEY

Let's follow this journey in your mind, starting at your feet and going all around the world, visiting places you're interested in, until you come back having completed a global circuit.

1. Notice where you come into contact with the ground right now. It may be that you are directly in touch with the earth, or more likely, your feet, or a chair's or bed's feet, are currently touching a floor.
2. This floor is connected to the building's walls and the foundations, where it's supported by and connected to the soil.
3. This soil at this building's foundations is part of the land that runs the entire length of this country, and somewhere near or distant, that land will end at the sea.
4. Here, the land that you're connected to, dives under the water and becomes the sea and ocean bed. It runs without a break beneath the ocean, maybe rising out of the water occasionally as islands, and finally leaving the ocean as it forms the shore and land of a distant continent.

5. Follow it across those continents and seas and continue onward until you arrive back where you began.

SPACE

Shift your focus now to the space above you. Astronomers and cosmologists tell us that every element in our body, the Carbon, Nitrogen, Oxygen, Hydrogen, Magnesium, Potassium and so on, originated about 13 billion years ago as the debris of exploding stars somewhere in the distant universe and, to quote the cosmologist Carl Sagan[41], 'we are all made of Star-Stuff'. Gravitational and relativity theories tells us that every object in the universe exerts some pull on every other part of the universe, affecting how it moves to a tiny or huge degree. This includes the way light is bent by massive objects, in the case of super dense 'black holes' affecting light so much that it cannot escape its pull (that's why they appear black), to the way the water on earth is pulled by the changing position of the moon, producing monthly variations in tides. To bring us back down to earth, this connection shows up in the words we use; 'month' has its origins in the word for the moon from the Greek (mēn) and Latin (mensis) (a lunar month lasts 27 days) and it also provides the origin for the 'menstrual' cycle (average 28 days), with some research suggesting there is synchronisation between those two cycles[42].

SPACE JOURNEY

1. Imagine sensing the connection between you and the space above you, by focusing, to start with, on the air that is just above your head.
2. Follow a path through that air, upwards and outwards. Track upwards past the height of a house (about 12m), go ten times higher to above a tall city skyscraper (150m), then six times higher to above the world's tallest building, currently the Burj Khalifa, Dubai (829.8 m). Then fifteen times higher to the height that commercial aeroplanes fly (at 12,000 m), then six times farther to the edge of the planet's atmosphere (at 80,000 m).

3. Go beyond that to the space that contains our moon (384,400 km away), through the solar system with its planets (furthest is Neptune at 4,351 million km) and the sun (150 million km away).
4. Imagine continuing onward to the collections of other planetary systems that form the vast galaxies.
5. And then imagine floating out into distant deep space, before heading back...
6. Through the galaxies, our solar system, our atmosphere, the space above you, and back to you.

NATURE AND TIME

Many of us have experienced a deep connection with something bigger than ourselves in the presence of nature. This may be observing a beautiful sunrise or sunset, standing inside a forest of ancient trees, or gazing at the sea that rolls gently in and out. We may get a sense that these experiences have been the same for hundreds of thousands of years before we arrived and will continue for many more hundreds and thousands of years. We may consider that our ancient ancestors stood gazing at these same wonders, maybe feeling as we do now. There is a Japanese word for something similar to this, Yūgen (幽玄), which is described as an awareness of the universe that brings on emotions that are too deep and powerful to be entirely captured by words.

NATURE AND TIME JOURNEY

- Re-immerse yourself in one of those moments of connection with nature that may come with that appreciation of a larger sense of time. Notice what you see, hear, feel and sense as you connect with that.

PLACES AND OTHERS

It may be that we've felt a deep and instant connection with another person, a special place, a particular animal, or pet that sparked something deep inside of us. Maybe it was a sense of belonging, coming home, being reunited, being part of something together, or feeling something deeply familiar. If you've had these experiences, you'll know how strong and moving these feelings of connection can be.

PLACES AND OTHERS' JOURNEY

- If you've had this experience, take a few moments to re-immerse yourself in that sense of deep connection. Noticing what you see, hear, and feel as you reconnect with this experience. Breathe that feeling into every part of you, noticing how the world feels different, how boundaries seem to blur, and how we can feel a sense of oneness with others when we start from this place of connection.

This IWT gives you a range of ways to experience the Gateway State of Connection which is an underused and unfamiliar state for many of us. However, once we start to experience the world as something we are part of rather than something that is outside of us, it helps us to make a whole range of fascinating MAPP shifts and transformations that are central to developing IW.

US AND/OR NATURE

The eminent anthropologist and ecologist Gregory Bateson wrote extensively in the 1960s and 1970s on the importance of our connection to nature. He noted that if we see nature as separate from us, we will feel ok about exploiting it. He warned that the result of this disconnection from nature and access to advanced technology would be to 'die either of the toxic by-products of your own hate, or, simply, of over-population and overgrazing. The raw materials of the world are finite.'[43] He also considered that 'The major problems in the world are the result of the difference between how nature works, and the way people think.'[43] The architect and philosopher Buckminster Fuller wrote of the importance of recognising how much we depend on the earth for survival. He asked people to think of the earth as a spaceship and to recognise that this was the only one on which we could survive. That this unique spaceship had a crew, us, all living humans, whose job was to maintain the health and structure of the one and only available life raft hurtling through space. He hoped this 'MAPP shift' would encourage us to realise that this singular spaceship was essential for our survival, and that we needed to do everything we could to take care of this precious vessel. Half a century later, these wise academics' words seem as important as ever. Regaining our appreciation and connection with nature is an important part of developing IW both for ourselves and the planet. For us to destroy the habitat that is vital for our survival is not a sign of behaviours driven by wisdom.

IWT 19: The Rice Grain

There's a mindfulness meditation from Buddhism that asks you to pause as you eat your meal, and to reconnect with our place in the vast system of nature by mindfully considering where this food has come from.

You can practise this IWT next time you eat. Imagine, for example, you're eating a meal with rice. As you pause to consider where it's come from, following its journey to you. It may go something like this....

This grain of rice was once a tiny seed planted by a farmer who probably lives far from you, who you don't know, and may never meet. We can imagine the way the seed was first planted by her, then nurtured by rains and carefully watered; how the nutrients in the soil, the sunshine and shade, and the continued attention of our farmer helped it survive and flourish, so eventually it was ready for harvesting. But we can trace its journey in so many other ways. We can follow how it arrived at our farmer's field. How it was bought from a seed merchant, paid for by the money our farmer earned from the previous year's harvest. How that money changed hands many times on its journey. The rice merchant used it not only to buy supplies of rice but also to pay for its transportation, storage, and security. To buy the cats to protect the rice and catch the mice that might want to feast on it in the storehouses. To buy the beautiful clothes that he bought for the daughters he doted on... And those clothes have their own story. Travelling from factories where the textile workers wove the fabrics and others fashioned and stitched them into clothes. Following the trail of the fabric back to the cotton plant or the silkworms producing their fine thread. Or maybe to the factory that produced the polyester from the refined petrochemicals, extracted from deep underground reservoirs formed from long forgotten tiny aquatic organisms that swam in the same sunshine we know, over 65 million years … Or we could travel along the journey of the rice grain itself after it is harvested, collected, sold, and stored somewhere, snuggled up to other rice grains waiting, full of possibility; transported by mule, truck, and ship, experiencing the dust of the track, the fumes of the diesel engine, the roll of the sea, and the conversations of the workers and sailors carrying it across the world to where we live. It's unloaded, divided, weighed, packaged, and moved to the store you bought it from. Your payment feeds the families and fuels the dreams of the store owners. You carry it home, and it waits for its moment to be of use, planted, or served on your table.

When we pause to do this when we eat, following any part of that journey, we become present to the Connectedness of the systems we are part of. We recognise how much work is being put in by nature, and that includes the other people all over the world, to make this event, the arrival of the rice to our mouth, happen.

But nature does more than sustain, and make the survival of our species possible, it also has some surprising effects on our health and well-being.

Green Health

Being near nature tends to increase health through the easy access it provides to space to play, hike, exercise, etc., but the effects are more far-reaching than that. Just living close to nature has strong health benefits, as identified by a 2016 study of 121,000 women. It found that those living in the greenest areas were 13 % less likely to die of cancer and 34 % less likely to die from a respiratory illness than women living in the greyest/most non-green areas. Those with the most greenspace within 250m of their homes experienced the biggest effect, although if greenspace was within 1250m the results were quite similar[44,45].

Others have reported on how living near greenspace increases emotional and psychological health, including, happiness, mood, social interactions, memory attention span, and children's school performance

- along with stress reduction, depression, and ADHD[46].

Even the presence of trees on your street has an impact. A study in Canada in 2015 concluded that the presence of 10 or more trees on a street block, compared to those with none, had self-reported health benefits similar to a $10,000 annual salary raise, or moving to a neighbourhood with a $10,000 higher median income, or being seven years younger. Additionally, it found that living on a tree-lined block resulted in fewer reports of high blood pressure, obesity, heart disease, or diabetes[46].

Even connecting with images and memories of nature has a positive impact on our health. Studies have shown that gazing at pictures of natural scenery reduces your stress levels, increasing the activity of the calming and nurturing part of our nervous system (the parasympathetic system)[47,48] and nature/green space images produce this effect much more effectively than when shown urban/grey space scenes[49].

Blue Health

A range of studies have shown that living near blue space, which is the water/river/lake/ocean equivalent of green space, also has a significant impact on improving our physical and mental health and well-being, including reducing anxiety and depression, and elevating our mood, and improving blood pressure, sleep, and immune function[50].

A 2019 study from Exeter University of 26,000 people, found those living 1 km from the sea were 22 per cent less likely to have symptoms of a mental health disorder compared to those who lived 50k away[51]. A range of factors was suggested as the cause of this, such as improved air quality and increased opportunities for social contact and physical activity that blue space provides. It also appears that being near water provides strong stress-reducing, health and immune system benefits in several ways:

First is the sound of the sea, which many find relaxing, prompting researchers to explore the mechanisms behind this. They suggest that it's because the brain has a pattern recognition system designed for spotting danger. When it's presented with the meaningless, ideal blend of 'white noise' that waves have, it switches from high alert to calm as it recognises there is 'nothing to see here'[52].

Second, waterfalls, which have a similar calming white noise profile to waves, produce the same effect, but also directly improve immune system function, and reduce asthma and markers of inflammation, due to the number of ionised water droplets they produce[53–55].

Thirdly, the flat spaciousness of the ocean appears to calm a primitive danger-sensing part of our nervous system. In dense jungle or built-up areas, it's difficult to see danger coming, so our danger sensors need to be on alert much of the time. However, flat surfaces like oceans and plains make it easy to spot danger at a great distance, and because that gives us plenty of time to take evasive action, it's ok to be relaxed and wind down in these spaces[49].

Fourth, blue space affects our experience of pain. Researchers found that by just 'taking' a coastal walk via a virtual reality headset patients' experienced a reduction in pain during dental procedures[56].

Fifth, getting into the water is good for us. This is especially true for cold-water swimming. When undertaken safely, it has been shown to improve our blood pressure and hormonal function, reduce upper respiratory tract infections, and improve mood disorders and general well-being[57].

IWT 20: Get Out And Promises

Based on all the above, an important step in developing IW is to get out and reconnect with nature, both for our well-being and to remind us of how important it is to take care of the planet we rely on to survive. This may also provide a secondary benefit, an opportunity to take a break from the ever-present screens that we seem to have become dûing increasingly connected to. These amazing labour-saving devices appear to have a dark side, as researchers identify how much they can harm our physical and mental health[58–60]. There's even evidence that the presence of a mobile phone on the table during a conversation between two people reduces the quality of the conversation, the sense of empathy, closeness and …. Connection[61,62].

Plan to get out in nature using the valuable 'promise' strategy of:

1. Making a clear commitment: Avoid stating what you 'won't be doing' as neurologically, this makes *that* more likely to happen: 'I don't want to just get stuck in front of the screen all day' results in telling your brain to 'get stuck in front of the screen all day'. State what you will be doing 'I'm going for a walk by the sea'.

2. Be precise: 'I'm going for a 20-minute walk by the sea by myself'.

3. You might want to add a state: 'I am going to do this while feeling Curious/happy/ Connected/present to what's going on around me'. So, when in nature, avoid listening to podcasts, making calls, checking emails, posting nature scenes to Instagram or getting annoyed at the time you're wasting away from your desk. Those aren't great ways to reconnect you to nature.

4. Add a 'by when' date: This prevents it from slipping off your 'to-do' list. 'I'll have completed a 20-minute walk by the sea by myself, being Curious and present by this Wednesday at 6 pm'.

5. Check with yourself if that's doable, ask yourself, 'Knowing my schedule and what's already planned, does that fit?' If it doesn't, that's fine, just adjust it until it does fit. Planning to do something that you already know is unachievable isn't a sign of IW.

6. Tell someone else about it. Speaking it out loud starts to make it real. You might even ask them to be your accountability partner if you want. They can check in with you to make sure that you've delivered on your promise to yourself.

When you approach connecting to nature in this way, notice how much clearer your choice feels and how much easier it is to make it happen.

You can also use this 'promise' strategy for anything else that needs clear goal setting. If you have a to-do list with things on it that have been there for more than 2 months, you may be familiar with the sense of dûing burdened by them, and dûing thinking of them late at night when you should be sleeping. Applying this process almost seems magical, as it will transform these burdens into clearly defined goals that you'll find much simpler to achieve than you might have imagined. And then you can finally cross them off that list.

OTHERS

One part of nature and Connection that often needs some focus is that of dealing with other people. We know it is important to regain our sense of Connection with the bigger system of the world around us, and yet when we encounter some people who are part of that system, we seem to dû difficulty around them. The next chapter provides some valuable IWT to help you with these situations.

'Yugen (幽玄) – the awareness of the universe that brings on emotions that are too deep and powerful to be entirely captured by words.'

CHAPTER 21: DEALING WITH OTHERS

The next sections will equip you with some powerful IWTs to deal more healthily and compassionately with 'challenging' situations where others are involved. They are divided up into the types of issues we all commonly come across. As each person we connect with is unique and differs in numerous ways from us, this creates many opportunities for confusion, miscommunication, and emotionally surprising responses. Mastering ways to navigate your way through these troubled waters is the final important stop on your journey to IW. You can apply all the techniques in the book presented so far to such issues, but these extra techniques will provide some excellent and wise ways to change how you respond to others' unexpected behaviours.

WRONG AND RIGHT?

Our compulsion to evaluate things as 'right' and 'wrong' is strongly linked to our ideas about failure and feedback covered in IWT 16. To discover how much you dû this, check in with your thoughts over the course of today and notice how many of them are judging someone or something as good/bad or right/wrong. Here's a sample of the types of things you'll hear:

- Why are they wearing that?? (They are wrong for wearing it).
- Why didn't they take out the trash? (They are wrong for not taking out the trash).
- They said what!? (They are wrong for saying it).
- I can't believe they did that! (They are wrong for doing it).
- How do they think doing that is ok!? (They're wrong for doing that).
- You shouldn't do that, it's not nice. (Their moral compass is wrong).
- Look at the size of their portion. (They have taken the wrong amount).
- I can't believe they said it in that way, with that tone of voice! (They are wrong for saying it that way).

- It would be better to have met and talked it through, rather than just emailing. (They are wrong).

The chances are that over the course of a 30-minute period, unless you are already an ascended master, you will have spotted hundreds of these internal judgey conversations. This wastes a lot of time and brain energy and is often not that good for us, or the other people involved.

It's also a great example of neuroplasticity at work, as we are taught at an early age how to judge the behaviours of others as right or wrong. Our educational system, particularly in the early years, measures our success through right and wrong, examples include, '2+2=4 is right, but 2+2=5 is wrong', 'this is the right way to behave' and, 'it's wrong to steal'. There are some powerful benefits to instructing our citizens of the future in this way, but there are also some downsides. As soon as we dû judgments about others' behaviours as right or wrong we start to head towards conflict with them. If someone has a different set of beliefs, values, or opinions from ours, it can be easy to fall into the trap of deciding that **they** are wrong and **we** are right. This is because we spent a long time working out our MAPP of how the world works from some very thoughtful reflections on the experiences we've had; we've listened to experts, discovered what happens when we do this or that, and we've come up with a pretty good map of how the world works. From this extensive research, we are sure of our conclusions. So, if someone's wrong, then it's definitely them.

Notice how this divides the world into 'Us' (with us) and 'Them' (against us) and provides a sense of being separate, and Separation is the opposite of Connection.

OUR NUMBER 1 DISLIKE

When one person suggests that the other person, and therefore their MAPP, is 'wrong', it creates a huge problem. This accusation appears to be one of the things we dislike the most. Let's imagine it's a simple difference of opinion between which is better, A or B - it could be a local restaurant or a movie. You say, 'I think A is better than B' and they respond, 'Actually, I think B is much better, A isn't that good'. This can start to sound a lot like: 'Your judgement is wrong'. We now think that they are implying that we haven't thought it through properly and that our conclusions about the world are stupid, foolish, idiotic, or half-baked. Now it starts to sound like: 'How could you possibly think this nonsense about the world, are you a complete idiot?'. This interpretation feels offensive, we start to dû upset and angry. This has moved from a difference of opinion to a sense of being attacked on an identity level. It's suggesting that we, as a person, are not wise enough to make good sense of the facts. From experience, we know that this rarely results in us thanking them for their extraordinary insight and a change in our worldview. Instead, we come out fighting, defending our rational thinking and our MAPP of the world, rejecting their outrageous implication that we're stupid, and pointing out why they and their stupid MAPP is wrong. We can start dûing annoyed with, or become very critical of, them. Then, because this clash of maps is a two-way street, they may well respond similarly by dûing annoyed or criticising us for 'being wrong'. This process can escalate even more rapidly if A or B is about something we hold even closer to our hearts, such as a political, religious or moral stance.

REWIRING ANNOYED, HURT OR CRITICISED

Although we are well practised at dûing judging others and staying fixed and positional about who is right or wrong, it is possible to change this. Reducing it will decrease separation and conflict, and as we saw in Chapter 19 on Parts, it steals energy and rarely helps things improve. Think about a time you received some criticism or negative comment about you or your plans. Notice that sense that they were suggesting that you were wrong. Can you identify that it was fundamentally a clash of MAPPS? They thought/knew the world was a certain way, and you thought/knew it was different. And because we each have a slightly different MAPP there are so many opportunities for this to happen. In IWT 16 we looked at transforming failure into feedback with particular reference to when we have been dûing hard on ourselves. In this section, we're going to be looking at how to deal with people dûing criticising us or suggesting that we failed in some way. We'll also look at how to deal with situations where we want to dû lashing out, dumping on, or criticising others. It's useful to know how to deal with these situations for two reasons. First, they occur so frequently. Second, when we dû lashing out or criticising the other person, they try to protect their MAPP by dûing lashing out at us. I'm sure we can all recognise moments in our lives where we've ended up in an escalating argument for exactly these reasons. So, what is the solution to avoid such right and wrong judgements? It's applying the Simple, Big Question, 'Is this way of thinking useful for me?' that we discovered in IWT 8.

IWT 21: Moving From 'Right and Wrong'

First, choose something that you notice you have a 'right and wrong' judgement about. It could be someone else's criticism of you, dûing annoyed/hurt at someone else's behaviour, or using 'should' phrases, such as 'they shouldn't have said that'.

Get prepared as before. Find a chair or bed that is safe to comfortably stand on (if that's not possible see the notes at the end for alternative steps). Arrange the 'You' and 'Inner Coach' as usual with the chair/bed behind the Inner Coach position (see the grey square in the diagram). Stand in the 'You' position, making sure that there are about 2 metres of space in front of you, and take 5 deep, easy breaths. You'll be familiar with some of these steps from IWT 8.

1. In the 'You' position (shown by the dotted circle with the arrow pointing to the RIGHT in the diagram). Reconnect with the Gateway State of 'Connection'.
2. As before, using this diagram as a guide:
   a. Step into the space just in front of you (the solid-line circle) marked 'Inner Coach'.
   b. Then turn around 180 degrees so you are looking back towards the space you were just standing in (as shown by the arrow pointing to the LEFT).

You　　　Inner Coach

3. In this solid-line circle, you will be taking the role of the Inner Coach. See the 'You' still standing in that dotted-line circle right in front of you - in the 'You' position. Looking directly at the 'You' over there, say out loud, as you did with the Self-Kindness IWT 4:
    a. 'I'm so proud of you and all that you have achieved.'
    b. 'Like that time when you...' (List a few things that you know took a lot of effort from you to make happen).
    c. 'I see these qualities in you...' (List them)
    d. 'You're really good at...' (List a few stand-out examples of skills and abilities that you know you have. No one else is listening, so it's ok to say them out loud. Examples include being patient with kids/making fabulous soup/gardening/making friends, etc. but choose YOUR own).
    e. 'And I really like that about you.'
    f. 'I know you've had to deal with some stuff in your life, and you always keep going.
    g. 'I know, like everyone else, although you don't always get it right all the time, you always do your very best.'
    h. 'I think you are a truly amazing person.'
    i. 'You (add your name), are enough'.
    j. 'I love you.'
4. Step back into the 'You' in the dotted-line circle and feel how it feels to hear your Inner Coach say these things to you. Let this in, then take some time to enjoy those feelings of Self-Kindness and acknowledgement. Doing

these steps first will make it much easier to answer the Simple, Big Question coming up. Now turn your attention to the issue you've been focusing on from a 'right or wrong' perspective.

5. Step back to the Inner Coach and say to 'You':
   a. I know this has been something you've felt you couldn't or shouldn't let go.
   b. But it's hurting you to keep it.

6. Now climb up onto the chair/bed behind the Inner Coach. From this position, as before, you will see it very differently, with much less emotion and more rationality. Ask the 'You' over there the Simple, Big Question, **'Is this way of thinking useful for you?'** Another way of phrasing this is to ask, **'Is this your wisest choice?'**

7. Return to the 'You' position and notice your answer - it should be 'NO'*.

8. Step back to the chair/bed and ask, 'Is there anything useful that you need to learn from this, that helps your future, before you can let it go completely?'

9. Step back into 'You' and notice your answer. You might be surprised at what comes up from your IW. Take a few deep breaths as you allow yourself to absorb these important learnings into your body, gut, heart, and mind.

10. Finally, reconnect with the Gateway State of Connection again and feel it flowing through you and anyone else involved. Flowing through those old past events, softening, shrinking, blurring out and giving you a new, healthier perspective on those events. Freeing yourself to step into your life in a new way. Feel how this future feels as you explore it with this sense of ease and flow. Notice how you feel differently now.

Notes:

- If you aren't able to easily or safely access a suitable chair or bed, then you can imagine yourself being one floor above where you are and looking down.
- Step 7 - If it's 'Yes' you'll need to move on to the Parts IWT 17.

Once you've experienced this process a few times, you may find you can shortcut it by just asking the Simple, Big Question (**'Is this your wisest choice?'**). It is very powerful to recognise that the conflict you were about to get into was not going to help the situation. The next steps are to move forward on a new path by applying any of the approaches detailed from IWT 22 to IWT 29.

IWT 22: The Listening Tree

Start by choosing an issue you'd like to resolve where there is a difference of opinion, a clash of MAPPs that's left you dûing upset or annoyed, or feeling like you want to 'give someone a piece of your mind' or lash out at them. Put that issue to one side as you find a quiet space, sit down, and take a few deep breaths to get ready for wise change.

    1.   Once you're ready, read through the story below:

Once upon a time, there was a small village where, as can happen with neighbours and families living in close proximity, the inhabitants frequently fell into minor arguments with each other. However, the elders recognised that these small disagreements often became heated, vicious, and entrenched, spiralling out of control so that grudges were held for weeks, months, years or, in some cases, generations, and that this animosity and discord wasn't good for anybody.

The chief elder decided she had to find a solution to the issue and, as was the custom, went out alone, walking in the woods. There, deeply connecting with nature, she sought answers and, guided by the spirits, found herself in front of a tall, strong, deep-rooted tree. She paused and thought for a while, wondering why she had been brought here. Then it came to her.

She realised that when people aired their grievances with each other, laced with heated emotions, harsh words, and agitated gestures, it ended in conflict rather than thoughtful resolution. There had to be a different way.

She politely asked the tree if it would be happy to listen to people's problems, giving them a chance to offload the strong emotions that caused the spiralling arguments. The tree had been around for hundreds of years. It had seen many seasons come and go, weathered the deep winter snows, the springs' raging storms and tinder-dry summers. It had watched as generations of village children were born and learnt to walk and run in the shade of its canopy. It had seen them grow to have children of their own and mature to become elders themselves, passing their flame of knowledge to a new generation. The tree was a silent, constant, and ancient member of the village, and in all those years, it had seen it all. It naturally agreed to help by listening patiently and compassionately to anyone who came to offload to it.

Now, when a villager has an issue with a neighbour they don't rush to confront or lash out at the other person first. Instead, they visit the tree.

They shout and rail, and weep and complain and vent as much as they need to, as the tree patiently listens. Everything they say, it has heard many times before, but each time it treats it like this is the most important time and just listens with complete attention and Kindness. They, in turn, now realise that voicing that directly to the other person would have only inflamed and prolonged the situation and not moved life on in a better way. On the walk back to the village, having expressed their strong emotions there and left them to be carried on the tree's broad shoulders, feeling the presence of its ancient wisdom, they feel different.

Returning, they find they have either decided that this problem isn't as important as it seemed, and now that they've told it to the tree, it's time to simply let it go. Or they find that there is something that needs resolving with the other person. However, having vented to the endlessly patient tree, they now feel they can discuss it through thoughtful conversation.

When travellers visit the village, they instinctively feel something is different here. They can't put their finger on it at first, but after a while, they notice the lack of bickering, complaining, and cold silences that are familiar to other villages. They see the warmth, compassion, and understanding of a community connecting, respecting differences, and communicating. Finally, they inquire as to the cause of this unusual extraordinariness, 'Is it the guidance of the elders, the healing waters, or the fresh food diet?' No, they're told, it's because we have a Tree that listens.

2. Take a few moments to pause and reflect on this story and what it means to you. You're going to use the concept of the Listening Tree to let go of the emotions we feel around the issue you've chosen to work on, so you can move on from the issue or discuss it in a calmer, more rational way with the others involved. You can either do this outdoors with a real tree or at home, picturing the tree in front of you. If staying inside, then I'd recommend finding and saving an image of a tree that looks like the one in the story and setting it as a desktop or screensaver image. Or if you prefer, draw it yourself and keep it somewhere you can easily see it daily. If you are happy to do this outside, then find a tree to talk to. When you're ready, continue with these steps.

3. When no one is listening (except the tree), turn to the tree or picture it in your mind, and begin to tell it everything you want to say to that other person. Fully express, talk, shout, vent, and get this out of your system. Let the tree take it all in and hear you. Continue until you feel you are 'done', you will know

you've achieved this when the emotions feel 'faded out, let go of, gone, softer, etc.'

4. Now get in touch with the Gateway State of Connection using any of the guided journeys in IWT 18.

5. Step into your Inner Coach space, which you should now be quite familiar with, and ask, 'Can you let this go now or do you need to calmly discuss this with the other person?'

6. Step into 'You' and answer.

7. Step into your Inner Coach space and ask if there are any other Gateway States that you need right now (Trust, Compassion, Curiosity, Shift, Transformation).

8. Step into 'You' and answer and get in touch with any Gateway States as required.

9. Finally, reconnect with the Gateway State of Connection again and feel it flowing through you and anyone else involved. Flowing through those old past events, softening, shrinking, blurring out, and distancing those events. Freeing yourself to step into your life in a new way. Feel how this future feels as you explore it with this sense of ease and flow. Notice how you feel differently now.

OTHERS IN THE 'WRONG' STATE

When resolving issues with others, we can see how important it is for us to choose the most useful state, either one of recognising it's time to let this go or staying calm when we rationally discuss the issue. If we're not dûing the most helpful state, then it may be useful to pause, take some time out, and come back to that conversation when you're in a better space.

There is, of course, another factor to consider, which is, what state is the other person dûing. It's important to remember that we cannot be in charge of another person's state. We may want them to dû calm or rational, but they may not want or feel able to dû that right now?

So how do we manage a situation where the other person is not dûing the 'best' state for that moment. Watch out for these classic 'pour petrol on the fire' moves that can make a problem even worse.

Firstly, although it may be tempting, avoid dûing blaming them for being in the 'wrong' state. Examples include 'There's no talking sense to you when **you're like this**, I'll come back when **you've calmed down'**. Note how we've placed all the blame on *their* inability to manage their state. If you feel like blaming them, then you're dûing annoyed and not in the best state either. Instead, take responsibility for your state, as covered in the earlier sections on responsibility and choice. A good way to say this is, 'I'm not sure I'm in the best place to talk this through calmly, in the way I want to. Can you give me a few minutes to get myself together, so I can come back to this from a better place?' Then calmly remove yourself and regroup using any of the IWT that will help you get into the state you need to be in.

RIGHT TIME?
You can add to this with an additional question, which can be particularly useful when dealing with teenagers or managing difficult conversations. A great starting point is to ask, 'Is this a good time to talk about this, as I'd love for us to find a way through this together?' If they say 'No' then the wise advice is to, yep, not talk about that thing with them right now.

Instead, end by saying, 'Ok, can you let me know when it's good to talk about this, as I'd love for us to find a way through this together?' If you try to force that conversation when the other person is in the wrong state, then you probably won't get very far in terms of resolving it. You're also likely to get yourself even further into the wrong state, and remember, when two people are dûing the wrong state, the conversation generally doesn't work very well.

COMPARISONS AND GRATITUDE
A further damaging consequence of our tendency to dû judging is that it often leads to the popular pastime of comparing ourselves to others. Deciding who's better, thinner, richer, happier, more successful, etc.

than us...

Research from the world of social comparison theory suggests that this is almost universally a bad thing[63]. There are two major forms of comparison, one is upward comparison, where we compare ourselves to others who have more of what we want, for example, more money, better clothes, or a nicer house. Unfortunately, this often leaves us dûing annoyed and frustrated that we don't have what others do. This focus on looking at how other people are doing also prevents us from dûing present to what we have ourselves and reduces our sense of gratitude for the good in our lives. This lack of being grateful for what you have also reduces happiness, fulfilment, health and well-being [64].

The other option is downward comparison, where we compare ourselves to those who have less than us. Very often, this results in seeing them as less than us, rather than as equals, in an attempt to feel better about ourselves. This also, unsurprisingly, is not linked to great mental well-being [65].

So, if you find yourself dûing comparing yourself to others or comparing this moment to another moment in the past or future, as many of us dû, pause and ask yourself again that simple, big question from IWT 21, 'Is this my wisest choice?'. You can then shift how you feel about those others, or past events, even more by moving on to the next IWTs.

IWT 23: Transforming Comparisons
In this IWT we can shift the focus of our comparison to make it healthier.

Take something or someone you have been dûing comparison about.

Get prepared in the usual way. Make sure there is about 1 metre of space in front and to the side of you. Stand in the 'You' position and take 5 deep, easy breaths.

1. In the 'You' position (shown by the dotted-line circle), reconnect with the Gateway States of Kindness and Connection.
2. We'll use the diagram from IWT 16: Failure to Feedback as a guide:
    a. Step into the space just in front of you (the solid-line circle) marked 'Inner Coach'.
    b. Then turn around 180 degrees so you are looking back towards the space you were just standing in (as shown by the arrow pointing to the LEFT).

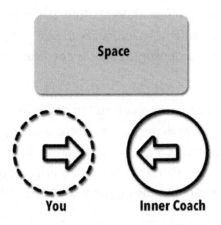

You   Inner Coach

3. Take the role of the Inner Coach. See the 'You' still standing in that dotted-line circle right in front of you - in the 'You' position. Looking directly at the 'You' over there, say out loud, as you did the Self-Kindness IWT 4:
    a) I'm so proud of you and all that you have achieved.'
    b) 'Like that time when you...' (List a few things that you know took a lot of effort from you to make happen).
    c) 'I see these qualities in you...' (List them)

d) 'You're really good at...' (List a few stand-out examples of skills and abilities that you know you have. No one else is listening, so it's ok to say them out loud. Examples include being patient with kids/making fabulous soup/gardening/making friends, etc. but choose YOUR own).

e) 'And I really like that about you.'

f) 'I know you've had to deal with some stuff in your life and you always keep going.'

g) 'I know, like everyone else, although you don't always get it right all the time, you always do your very best.'

h) 'I think you are a truly amazing person.'

i) 'You (add your name), are enough'.

j) 'I love you.'

---

4. Step back into the 'You' in the dotted-line circle and feel how it feels to hear your Inner Coach say these things to you. Let this in, then take some time to enjoy those feelings of Self-Kindness and acknowledgement. Doing these steps first will make it much easier to move through the next steps. Now turn your attention to the issue you've been dûing 'comparison' about and start to resolve it by placing it in the 'Space' to your left.

5. Step back to the Inner Coach and, pointing to the issue in the 'Space', say to 'You', 'I know this is something you've found difficult to deal with, and I really get that.'

6. Step back into 'You' and notice how that feels to have your Inner Coach on your side, understanding what's been going on for you.

7. Step back to the Inner Coach and point to the issue in the 'Space' and ask the following questions - stepping back into 'You' after each one and noticing your answers. You might be surprised at what comes up from your IW:

    a. For upward comparisons (the 'they're doing better than me' type phrases):

      i. 'What can you learn from this that is inspiring and empowering?'

      ii. 'What do you need to be or know to be at peace and accepting of this, while finding your own path?'

      iii. 'If they can achieve that, what can you achieve?'

      iv. 'Who do you need to be to use this for good?'

  b. For downward comparisons (the 'I'm doing better than them' type phrases):

      i. 'How can you support them in their journey?'

      ii. 'What do you now see that you can be grateful for?'

      iii. 'Who do you need to be to use this for good?'

---

8. Then as the Inner Coach ask, 'What Gateway State, or other state, would help you move through this in the most empowered way?'

9. Step back into 'You' and notice which state will be most useful. Take yourself back to a time when you deeply experienced this in the way you've practised throughout the book. Take a few deep breaths as you deeply connect with the powerful state you've chosen. Allow yourself to absorb this feeling into your body, gut, heart, and mind.

10. In a moment, this 'powered up' 'You' and your Inner Coach are going to step together in, and through, that 'Space' that represents the comparison issues you used to dû stuck with. Feeling that state you chose in step 10 and reconnecting with WHO you are going to be, turn towards the 'Space' and step in, and through it. Hear, see, imagine, and feel the presence and support of your Inner Coach walking next to you. Notice how it feels to move in this

new way through this area of your life that used to dû stuck.

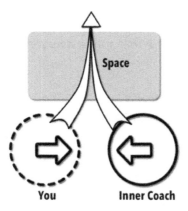

11. Step beyond it, to the head of the arrow, with your Inner Coach beside you, and look back, how does it feel to see and experience this change?
12. Staying here, reconnect with the Gateway States of Kindness and Connection again and feel them flowing through you and anyone else involved. Flowing through those old places where you used to dû stuck and healing those moments. Flowing into your future with these new states and an empowered sense of who you are. Notice how you feel differently now.

Notes:

* This quality of knowing you are enough is the antidote to the issues that can arise from comparison.

As comparison is such a common habit, being able to switch from a focus of unhealthy comparison to one of empowerment, learning and Kindness is one of the key steps to developing IW and a central part of connecting to the Gateway State of Connection.

IWT 24: Celebrate difference

We now understand how conflict occurs when our MAPP clashes with another person's. This IWT provides a great way for resolving conflict with others and reduces the importance of comparisons. It focuses on how we can change our MAPP that states 'everyone needs to share the same MAPP'.

Begin by getting into the Gateway State of Curiosity. Then consider how you feel about people who differ from you. For many of us, we don't find it that comfortable, they can seem strange, and it's odd to think they have a completely different version of the world from us.

Let's explore a different MAPP. I invite you to Curiously imagine a world where everybody did agree about everything.

In that world, as everybody would like the same tastes and flavours there would be very few food choices in stores or restaurants; the TV shows would all be the same because everybody enjoys the same kind of thing; conversations would be quite tedious and predictable: 'What did you think about that film?', 'I liked it'... 'So did I'. There would be no discussions or debates, no differences of opinion or intriguing discoveries of unfamiliar ways of thinking about the world; no thought-provoking art, books, or new thinking that opens up novel ideas; only a limited range of music would be available, as there would only be a demand for a narrow range of artists; clothes would be identical across generations, all in the same colours and styles, themes that would be replicated in everything from our house décor, newspapers, magazines and cereal packaging to the cars we drive. Everything would be pretty much identical. Surprisingly, a world where there is no difference and universal agreement, something we might have thought we wanted, would make for a very dull world.

What if we could be present to this when we discover differences and remain Curious and intrigued, wondering what we might learn or discover? What does that feel like to bring this to a difference of opinion that shows the presence of a new MAPP?

What if we also brought compassion and acceptance to these experiences?

Using these approaches to stop our instant reaction of 'their MAPP of the world is wrong' so we can stay in communication with these people with a different view may lead to fascinating new experiences and perspectives. When we can do this with a sense of Kindness and Curiosity, we can remain connected despite our differences. We have a chance, then, to be open to newness and to the idea that maybe our own MAPP isn't the only one available and that there may be updates to it that improve our understanding of the world.

Acceptance And Indifference

The previous section mentioned an interesting and powerful state, that of 'Acceptance'. It's invaluable for dealing with difference, as it's the opposite of viewing things as 'right or wrong'. It describes the ability to be OK with the fact that things are the way they are. Even if they are not as you expected them to be, it fits well with the Gateway State of Curiosity, the ability to be intrigued by things you didn't expect. You may also recall, it showed up in the earlier section on Serenity. It's especially valuable when dealing with others' unexpected or unwanted behaviours, as we know we don't have the power to directly make them change.

There's another state that can be equally useful when dealing with others, that of 'Indifference'. It's feeling as though others' behaviours and actions are of no great consequence or interest to you.

To prepare for the next IWT let's access the states of Acceptance and Indifference.

Acceptance

Think of a time when you were accepting of something that you wished wasn't the way it was. It could be a minor thing, such as wanting a particular dish at a restaurant only to find it wasn't on the menu that day, or a friend having to cancel dinner plans because of illness. These are things you would rather hadn't happened, but they did, and you were able to move beyond them. Pick an example that is a good example of you accepting things that were not the way you wanted them to be.

Indifference
Think of something that, for you, has no positive or negative meaning, but for someone else, it might be really important. For example, a friend is a huge fan of a particular food - say truffles. You don't love or hate them, you can take it or leave them. When they invite you to join them on a tasting holiday focused entirely on truffles, you think it would be ok, but it's not your dream holiday. You can choose to join in or not, it depends on what other potential holiday options there are to choose from.

IWT 25: Judging And Upset To Acceptance Or Indifference
Take something or someone you have been dûing judging or upset about.

Get prepared in the usual way. Make sure there is about 1 metre of space in front and to the side of you. Stand in the 'You' position and take 5 deep, easy breaths.

1. In the 'You' position (shown by the dotted-line circle), reconnect with the Gateway States of Kindness and Connection
2. We'll use the diagram from IWT 16: Failure to Feedback again as a guide:
   a. Step into the space just in front of you (the solid-line circle) marked 'Inner Coach'.
   b. Then turn around 180 degrees so you are looking back towards the space you were just standing in (as shown by the arrow pointing to the LEFT).

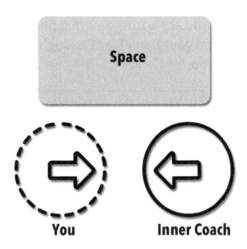

3. Take the role of the Inner Coach. See the 'You' still standing in that dotted-line circle right in front of you - in the 'You' position. Looking directly at the 'You' over there, say out loud, as you did the Self-Kindness IWT 4:

    a. 'I'm so proud of you and all that you have achieved.'

    b. 'Like that time when you...' (List a few things that you know took a lot of effort from you to make happen).

    c. 'I see these qualities in you...' (List them)

    d. 'You're really good at...' (List a few stand-out examples of skills and abilities that you know you have. No one else is listening, so it's ok to say them out loud. Examples include being patient with kids/making fabulous soup/gardening/making friends, etc. but choose YOUR own).

    e. 'And I really like that about you.'

    f. 'I know you've had to deal with some stuff in your life and you always keep going.'

g. 'I know, like everyone else, although you don't always get it right all the time, you always do your very best.'
h. 'I think you are a truly amazing person.'
i. 'You (add your name), are enough'.
j. 'I love you.'

4. Step back into the 'You' in the dotted-line circle and feel how it feels to hear your Inner Coach say these things to you. Let this in, then take some time to enjoy those feelings of Self-Kindness and acknowledgement. Doing these steps first will make it much easier to move through the next steps. Now turn your attention to the issue you've been dûing 'judging or upset' about and start to resolve it by placing it in the 'Space' to your left.
5. Step back to the Inner Coach and pointing to the issue in the 'Space' and say to 'You', 'I know this is something you've found difficult to deal with, and I really get that.
6. Step back into 'You' and notice how that feels to have your Inner Coach on your side, understanding what's been going on for you.
7. Step back to the Inner Coach and point to the issue in the 'Space' and ask, 'What states do need to resolve this, Acceptance or Indifference?'*.
8. Step back into 'You' and notice which states will be most useful. Take yourself back to a time when you deeply experienced one of these states in the way you've practised throughout the book. Take a few deep breaths as you deeply connect with the state/s you've chosen. Allow yourself to absorb this feeling into your body, gut, heart, and mind.
9. In a moment, this 'powered up' 'You' and your Inner Coach are going to step together in, and through, that 'Space' that represents the judging or upset issues you used to dû stuck with. Feeling that state you chose in step 8, turn towards the 'Space' and step in, and through it. Hear, see,

imagine, and feel the presence and support of your Inner Coach walking next to 'You'. Notice how it feels to move in this new way through this area of your life that used to feel stuck.

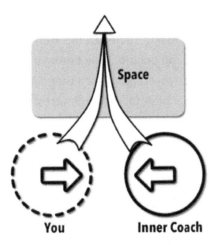

10. Step beyond it, to the head of the arrow, with your Inner Coach beside you, and look back. How does it feel to see and experience this change?
11. Staying there, reconnect with the Gateway States of Kindness and Connection again and feel it flowing through you and anyone else involved. Flowing through those old places where you used to dû judging or upset and healing those moments. Flowing into your future with these new states and an empowered sense of who you are. Notice how you feel differently now.

Notes:

- You can choose both states. Run the process from step 8 to 11 using one state (most people choose to work with indifference first) and then repeat that section with the second state.

1ST, 2ND, 3RD AND ZERO POSITIONS

In this section, I'll introduce a fascinating concept called 'Perceptual Positions'.

The numbers 1st, 2nd, 3rd, and Zero identify the different roles and perspectives we can have in an event. As an overview, the '1st position' represents the point of view of seeing things from our own perspective, or our own MAPP. The '2nd position' is where we view the world from someone else's perspective, stepping into their MAPP. In the '3rd position' we take the role of detached, uninterested observer, watching the interactions of other people. The 'Zero' position is the Gateway State of Connection that's been our focus in these chapters. These different positions allow us to perceive and re-process events from multiple different perspectives, and understanding them will provide great access to IW. There's also a powerful IWT that uses them based on Robert Dilts' Meta Mirror Pattern[66]. First, let's explore the first three positions, where they can be useful and where they can cause issues through overuse or underuse.

1ST POSITION

This is the perceptual position where we are focused on what **we** think about things, and what our needs, feelings, and experiences are. Here we see the world from our own MAPP or point of view. We are less concerned about others' needs or experiences, although we may guess, judge, and evaluate how their thoughts or behaviours might affect us.

We probably start out life from this perspective, since, as infants our focus is mostly on our own needs and experience. 3 months old babies rarely worry about upsetting their parents by screaming for attention in the middle of the night when **they need** something. These early experiences may result in this perspective being a starting point for how many of us experience the world.

As we'll see for all three positions, each one can provide great value, but accessing them too much or too little of the time, or at unhelpful times, can cause issues.

Useful: Being in position one is so valuable when you are thinking about what you want, what your choices, dreams, or goals are, what is, or is not, OK for you, and what you are prepared to accept and tolerate. It can be valuable for pioneers and those going against the usual way of doing things.

Overuse: People who spend too much time in 1st position are likely to have less insight into how things are for other people because they're only seeing the world from their own point of view. 1st Position can be great for working out what you want, but when overused, it can make you insensitive to other people's needs or responses to how you're being. Dictators, narcissists, and bullies see the world in 1st position most, if not all, of the time.

Underuse: Those who don't spend time in 1st position when they need to, for example, when making choices about their lives, can end up feeling that they don't know what they need or want and start to rely on other people to tell them. This can result in a life that's planned by others that's rarely fulfilling, a sense of disempowerment, and a loss of their sense of self.

Ask yourself: How am I using 1st position? Am I clear about what I want and what my goals are? Do I override others too much, and not see things from their point of view enough? Or do I listen too much to others?

2ND POSITION

This position involves seeing a situation that you are involved in, from somebody else's point of view. If it's a disagreement, for example, you will take the perspective of the person that you are arguing with.

Useful: This can be invaluable in understanding how others are feeling and resolving arguments and conflict. It helps in seeing things in a new light, encouraging creative processes, and sensing how you and situations show up for somebody else. It's invaluable for creating rapport and great relationships and for insightful, intuitive therapy and coaching.

Overuse: Spending too much time viewing the world from other people's perspectives can make you over-aware of other people's needs, forget what's important for you, and put their needs above yours to the detriment of your own well-being. This is often combined with underusing 1st position. This may result in a poor sense of self, low self-worth, and falling into co-dependent, controlling, and coercive friendships or relationships.

Many who are drawn to caring for others, either in a paid or unpaid capacity, are likely to be skilled at 2nd position. This can have negative side effects, as they can become so aware of how something feels for others, start to take on others' emotions or symptoms or feel compelled to rescue them and fix their world for them. This rescuing/fixing approach rarely works, and disempowers the person they are 'helping' as it reinforces that they are not capable of solving this without help, and can result in 'the carer' burning out from exhaustion.

It's also common among parents, particularly mothers, who find they are still shouldering much of the childcare responsibilities. This imbalance is supported by data from the UK where, of those with children, men spent 39 per cent of the time that women spent on childcare [67]. As a result of caring for their youngsters, parents can find there's little time left for themselves. If this situation continues, they can forget that 'me time' is important, as everything else like homework, cooking, cleaning, tidying up, (yep, all the fun things) etc. have to come first. The consequences of this aren't good. They may dû frustrated, stressed, resentful, or burnt out. Parenting and relationships can suffer and as children often learn their behaviours from the adults around them, it may be setting up more of the same for the next generation. This underlines how important making time for themselves and creating a balance between 1st and 2nd position is for parents and their children's futures.

Underuse: This can produce a sense of disconnection from other people, as they may lack insight into how things are for the other person. They can seem like they don't care or understand, and they may appear cold, insensitive, or too wrapped up in their own stuff to have time or attention for others.

Ask yourself: Am I good at sensing others' moods and emotions? Am I over-empathetic, feeling everything they feel? Do I spend more time thinking about the needs of others than my own? Do people tell me I'm cold and unaware of their feelings? (Note in this last one that your insight will come from people letting you know rather than you sensing it, as, if you're not in 2nd position, you won't be 'aware' of it, because you'd need to be stepping into them to realise that.)

3RD POSITION

In this perceptual position, we take the role of an unbiased observer.

Useful: Taking this position when there are emotions that are difficult to hold or when resolving conflict allows us to calmly observe what is occurring in an emotionally detached way. This, and the wider perspective it gives us, help us to gain rational and nuanced insights and find innovative solutions.

Overuse: Over-occupying the observer position can make us unemotional, disconnected, and feel like a bystander in our own life who is not 'present'. Signs include; others telling you that you are over-analytical, hyper-sceptical; running the 'yes, but' pattern (responding to helpful suggestions by immediately seeing the problems); or finding it difficult to imagine or reconnect with powerful states. Certain careers can encourage this way of thinking, so it may be more prevalent in some researchers, architects, lawyers, and journalists.

Underuse: Finding it difficult to step out of 1st and 2nd positions can prevent us from having this more nuanced way of perceiving situations. Professionals who deal with emotionally charged situations need to use 3rd position to effectively step away from the emotional impact of their work or client situations. It's also useful for reflecting on and improving how they work. Without good access to 3rd position, people can end up being unreflective and emotionally entangled with their work or clients' emotions.

Ask yourself: Do I find it easy to step away from difficult emotions, or do I find myself getting sucked into feeling everything? Do people think I'm cold, emotionally unavailable, detached, or overanalytical?

EXPLORING THESE POSITIONS
Some of these perspectives will be more familiar to you than others. Developing a familiarity with all the positions is an essential part of IW.

1. Start by becoming aware of which positions are most unfamiliar and which you favour.
2. Work to develop a familiarity with all the positions by practising and trying each one on in different situations. The next IWT will help with this.
3. When you've practised this enough, you'll find that you can make useful choices about which one you need to be in for the situation that you're dealing with currently.

IWT 26: Shifting Relationships
This IWT provides an excellent way to change stuck behaviours we dû around others and transform difficult relationships. It uses the 3 perceptual positions above as well as the zero position and the Gateway States.

Find a quiet space in a room that would be large enough to easily fit a bed in. Begin by choosing a troubled relationship to work on and note the situation or memory that is still causing you to dû problems. This IWT can also be used for relationships that no longer exist but, because the issues remain unresolved, can still cause upset. Often, an old, difficult relationship may be influencing current relationships with people who remind you of that person from the past. As a result, resolving the old issues can free you to respond differently to current relationships. As usual, pick a mild example to start with.

As a brief reminder, the three positions are:

1st Position is you being you: ME (Position 1 in the diagram)

2nd Position is stepping into the shoes of the other person in the relationship: THEM (Position 2 in the diagram)

3rd Position is taking the role of an observer: OBSERVER (Position 3 in the diagram)

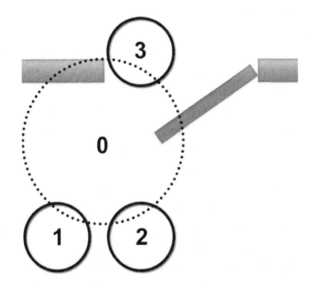

1. Place three pieces of paper on the floor, as shown in the diagram. 3 is some distance from 1 and 2. If you can use a doorway, place position 3 just outside the slightly open door, so it's not in the same room as 1 and 2.
2. Begin by choosing a specific incident that still contains some emotional upset. Step into position 1 and ask, **'What do I see, think, and feel about 'them'?'** The purpose of this is to find out where you are in terms of this stuck relationship. Naturally, we don't spend too long in this state, as it is

usually not a very useful one, but it will help us measure change at the end. Shake that off and move to position 2.

3. In position 2, ask, **'What do I see, think, and feel about '1'?'** Make sure you describe it using the 'other person's' words, as if you were that other person. So, if it's an issue between you (1) and Jo (2), when you move to position 2, you describe how 'Jo feels about you', using the words Jo would use, e.g., 'I don't like the way they treat me. I think they're rude and ungrateful'. Many find that by taking this second position, they gain some fascinating and life-changing insights about themselves.

4. Move to position 3 being a disinterested observer, watching these two strangers (if you can, look at them through the half-opened door). Taking this 3rd position provides new and impartial insight into what's going on. Make sure you really take an unbiased observer's position; you don't know these people, or their history, you can only guess at what's going on from what they observe.
   a. Ask, **'What do I make of this?'** Answer out loud.
   b. Observing from this position, ask yourself, **'What Gateway States does 1 need?'**. Note the answers.

5. When you have a list of 2-3 states, take one step forward from position 3, and there, recall and reconnect with those states. Now beam them into the 'You' in position 1.

6. Now step back into position 1 and feel how it feels with these new qualities. Notice how that changes how you feel about that other person (in 2)

7. Step back into position 2. Notice how 'You' (in 1) look different to them too.

8. Step back into position 1 and discover how different it feels now.

9. Finally, step into position Zero (the space between 1,2 and 3) and connect with the Gateway State of Connection. It's not being in you (position 1), the other (position 2) or observer (position 3), but instead being a part of everything. Here, there is no sense of me, you, or them as separate

entities, and time itself seems to blur and be perceived differently. Breathe deeply as you connect into this position zero and feel how coming from this perspective naturally further transforms this situation on a deeper level.

10. As you connect with these new understandings and perspectives, feel how different it feels to flow through an interaction with this person, or someone like them, in the future. Notice your new internal conversations, your sense of calm and confidence, and how differently you respond to them. Take yourself forward in time to when you have successfully sailed through this kind of thing hundreds of times. How does that deepen how familiar and confident you are in dealing with these kinds of situations and interactions? And how does that develop your sense of *who* you are?

SAYING NO

In the section on perceptual positions, the pattern of dûing worry about other people and their opinions often shows up. It underlies the issues of comparison and dûing worry about getting things 'wrong', as these are often driven by the concern of, 'What will others think of me if I did that?'.

Having no concept of other opinions (dûing 1st position all the time) is not great for us or others, as we become thoughtless and ignore others' perspectives. But dûing over-concerned about what others think (overusing 2nd position) is just as damaging. One of the consequences of overusing 2nd position is dûing a fear of saying 'NO' as we can imagine 'how upset someone might be' or may feel we're not helping them as much as we 'should'. This results in us doing things we don't want to do and having no time to do things we need or want to do for ourselves.

In itself, saying 'YES' to others' requests is not a bad thing. There are times when we do need to do things we don't particularly want to do, such as paying our taxes, and times when saying yes is inconvenient for us but important as someone needs our help, but it has to be combined with a sense of thoughtful, wise choice.

Asking additional questions will help this process. These include:

- Do I have the time and energy to do this?
- If I do this, would I still be able to do the other things that are important?
- Is this a wise use of my time?
- Do I want to do this?
- Could they do this themselves?
- Am I doing this because I've thought it through and made a clear, wise choice, or is this coming from a fear of what they will think about me if I don't do it?

These checks and balance questions help us get clear about whether this is one of the requests or invitations, we will accept, or, this time, we won't.

It can be useful to create a pause by saying, 'I just need some time to check what my other commitments are, and then I'll get back to you'. This gives us a chance to interrupt the unthinking knee-jerk response of 'yes of course I'll do it' and to consider whether this is one of those times when we will say yes or one of these times when we will pass.

When people make these new healthier choices around saying 'YES' or 'NO' it can be very interesting to observe how others respond to this change. Supportive friends will be pleased that we are making choices about our lives and how we spend our time. It's very revealing if we get some pushback from others who suggest that by saying 'NO' we have become 'uncaring, thoughtless, or selfish'. This identifies that the 'friend' has been benefiting from having an unpaid staff member working for them and is now quite annoyed that they will lose this free resource. This is their attempt to get us to change back to how we were before. This kind of response is often a sign that the relationship was not equal, balanced, or very healthy.

If you notice you avoid saying 'NO' then you'll find the presence of the strong and kind coach in the IWTs will be invaluable in changing this. Additionally, the IWTs that follow will transform this, and when you have moved on from dûing compelled to have to say 'YES', you will be so pleased that you freed yourself from this trap.

IWT 27: Wise Ancestor

This technique can be used to help you to say 'NO', but is also an approach that is useful for so many other issues as it helps you develop a deep connection with your IW from a new, yet ancient, perspective.

1. Get prepared as usual and find somewhere comfortable to sit. Consider an issue that you would like some assistance with, then take a few deep breaths.
2. Using the family tree diagram to help you visualise this, I'd like you to imagine a line that represents your past. This is your personal timeline.

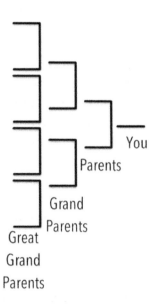

3. Follow it back in time in your mind's eye to around the time of your birth. There see two timelines, one for each of your parents. These lines stretch back in time, way

before you arrived. Follow them in your mind all the way back to *their* births. There, picture four further timelines, one for each of their parents. Follow this sequence backwards, doubling the number of lines at each generation. Just imagine 10 generations. Each generation represents about 25 years of time (between their birth and their child's birth). So, within 10 generations, you have gone back in time 250 years (to the 1770s as I write this). Would you like to guess how many direct parents/grandparents/great-grandparents, etc. you have in your family tree at this point? It's 1,024. And at 20 generations (500 years ago)? It's over 2 million ancestors. Modern humans (*Homo Sapiens*, Latin for 'wise man') have been around since about 200,000 years ago, but their ancestors, Homo Erectus, a pretty sophisticated version of us, were walking around, about 1.9 million years ago. That's a whole lot of ancestors.

4. With that in mind, let your IW guide you as you find your focus drawn to one of your ancestors who would be considered to be very wise. They may be someone you directly know or someone you just sense must have existed in that vast array of humanity. It could be a wise woman who knew where the healing herbs could be gathered in the forest or who helped women to give birth successfully; it might be someone skilled in crafts who knew how to fashion wood or shape stones to make elegant and lasting structures; it might be a wise peacemaker, communicator, or diplomat; maybe a leader or someone who inspired others; an innovator who was the first person who tamed a wild horse, made friends with the wolves, understood how fire worked, discovered the seasons, planted seeds, mended a fracture, built a shelter, made music, or painted the walls of a cave. Take your time, let that wise ancestor appear in front of you, and notice how it feels to see and connect with them.

5. They are so pleased to see you, as you are their direct descendant. Everything they went through in their lives was worth it because you, and the intervening ancestors, got to live and breathe, and you are the evidence of that extraordinary journey of success. In a moment, this wise ancestor will turn to you and say something that is so important for you to hear at this moment in your life. You know those moments when you stumble across something, and it rings so true that you can't help but take it in on a deep level. Listen to what they say, let it repeat inside you, resonating through every part of your body. Notice how it feels, and how supportive and valuable their presence and wisdom are.

6. Take a few moments to ask them any questions that you would like their input on. Feel how it feels to have their wise counsel supporting and assisting you.

7. Enjoy the experience of connecting with this ancestor. Imagine what it's going to be like to have them join in as part of your Inner Coach from now on. Feel what it's like to have them walking with you, being a calm, solid, and stable presence alongside you on every step of your future.

IWT 28: MAGIC CARPET

Like the previous IWT 27, with the wise ancestor, this next technique looks at time in a different way than usual. This shifts how we feel about what's going on right now in our lives and puts everything in a more useful perspective. It can also be used for dealing with others, but like the previous IWT, because it provides a transformational shift in how we see things, it can be applied to such a huge range of issues. Get prepared as usual and find somewhere comfortable to sit. Consider an issue that you would like to see differently, then take a few deep breaths.

1. Picture a beautiful, intricately woven carpet, the kind you might find in the tales of Aladdin. And, of course, this one flies.

2. Imagine climbing onto it and feeling comfortably relaxed as the carpet gently rises. Thoughtfully, you look over the side, you can see 'you down there' and the period of time that you're living in gets smaller and smaller the higher you go, until the last 20 years take up only a few centimetres of space below you. The carpet begins to travel back in time, 2000 years into the past, to the time around the Western calendar's year zero. How much do you know about this period of time? You may be aware that the Romans were in power in Europe and the Middle East, or that Pontius Pilate was the Governor of Judea. Documents from after that date tell us that Jesus was crucified at this time, but that may just about be the extent of what most of us know about this time. Not much survives of the everyday experiences. The challenges, the causes of arguments or grudges, the troubles, gossip, births, deaths, losses, successes, who had the fanciest house, most beautiful partner, or fastest chariot. Little that seemed deeply important to those who lived in those times survives or was considered important enough to be recorded and remembered.

3. Now travel from that point to today. Then continue a further 2000 years into the future, to the year 4000. What do the people living in 4000 recall about the years around 2000? In the same way that we have few pieces of information about year zero, they probably recall very little. They may classify it as just a part of the 'electronic age' and may include, as we do with year zero, 200 years on either side. They may see the 2020s as being '1800 (the era of Napoleon and Beethoven) to 2200', as one single moment in time. And they may not know Napoleon or Beethoven - how many generals or composers do you know from 2000 years ago?

4. From this perspective in time, gaze back toward the 2020s, to the time you live in now. What will they remember? How important will all those arguments, slights, grudges, concerns, worries, or the things that keep you awake at night seem to them? How does going on this journey allow them to blur, shift their importance to you now, and transform your perspective on it all?

5. When you feel you've gained the insight you need from this journey, you can connect again with your ancient wise ancestor. As they join you on the magic carpet, listen to them and what they share with you as a result of this journey. Then return to the here and now, feeling differently, more settled, and more deeply at peace.

IWT 29: Connection With Your Mission

The final IWT focuses on the power of connection on a different level. We've connected to our Inner Coach, our wise ancestors, to other people in a healthy way, and even to everything in the universe! Now it's time to connect with what we are truly passionate about. Doing this is a vital part of living a great and wise life. It's one of the things that will get us up in the morning, make each day feel meaningful, and give us a sense of purpose and deep fulfilment.

Some people have a vague sense of what their mission is, others have a clear, strong vision, but most of us have a sense that there *is* something for us to do, some mission we need to complete in life. Let's begin the process of uncovering and reconnecting with your passion/mission with some powerful questions. Once you've considered these questions, you'll be ready to move on to using them with the Inner Coach.

Prepare yourself in the usual way, sit down with several sheets of paper something to draw or write with. Get in touch with the Gateway States of Trust and Curiosity and notice what your IW comes up with as you ask yourself these questions.

- What are you passionate about?

- What do you dû angry about because the world 'should not be that way'?
  - Sometimes identifying what we dû annoyed about can be a route to finding out what we feel needs to change in the world.
- What would you do for no reason other than you love it or it feels too important not to... ?
  - You'd do it even if there was no:
    - Financial reward
    - Praise or recognition
  - As just doing it and being on that path is enough.
- What would make you get up out of bed at 4 am on a wet, cold, windy morning? What is your 'WHY' that drives you to do this?
  - Nietzsche alludes to this when he writes, 'If we have our own **why** in life, we shall get along with almost any **how**.'
- What is it, that, when you think of it, the very idea of it excites you?
  - Although in some cases you might dû fear about how big or important it is too.
- What is it, that, if you knew you couldn't fail at it, you would do it tomorrow?
- What is the biggest, most important change you'd like to see in the world?

Now that you're focused on this important aspect of life, continue with the following steps.

Get prepared in the usual way. Make sure there is about 1 metre of space to your side and in front of you. Stand in the 'You' position and take 5 deep, easy breaths.

1. In the 'You' position (shown by the dotted-line circle), reconnect with the Gateway States of Curiosity and Connection.

2. We'll use the diagram from IWT 16: Failure to Feedback again as a guide:
   a. Step into the space just in front of you (the solid-line circle) marked 'Inner Coach'.
   b. Then turn around 180 degrees so you are looking back towards the space you were just standing in (as shown by the arrow pointing to the LEFT).

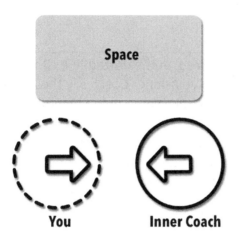

3. Take the role of the Inner Coach. See the 'You' still standing in that dotted-line circle right in front of you - in the 'You' position. Looking directly at the 'You' over there, say out loud, as you did the Self-Kindness IWT 4:
   a. 'I'm so proud of you and all that you have achieved.'
   b. 'Like that time when you...' (List a few things that you know took a lot of effort from you to make happen).
   c. 'I see these qualities in you...' (List them)
   d. 'You're really good at...' (List a few stand-out examples of skills and abilities that you know you have. No one else is listening, so it's ok to say them out loud. Examples include being patient with

kids/making fabulous soup/gardening/making friends, etc. but choose YOUR own).

    e. 'And I really like that about you.'

    f. 'I know you've had to deal with some stuff in your life and you always keep going.'

    g. 'I know, like everyone else, although you don't always get it right all the time, you always do your very best.'

    h. 'I think you are a truly amazing person.'

    i. 'You (add your name), are enough'.

    j. 'I love you.'

_____

4. Step back into the 'You' in the dotted-line circle and feel how it feels to hear your Inner Coach say these things to you. Let this in, then take some time to enjoy those feelings of Self-Kindness and acknowledgement. Doing these steps first will support your journey through the next steps. Think about whatever comes up for you when you think about your 'Mission' and place the 'Space' to your left.

    a. Step back to the Inner Coach and pointing to the issue in the 'Space' and say to 'You', 'I know this is important for you, and I'm going to support you in finding your way through it.'

5. Step back into 'You' and notice how that feels to have your Inner Coach on your side.

6. Step back to the Inner Coach and point to the issue in the 'Space' and ask, 'What states do you need to move forward with this?'

7. Step back into 'You' and notice which states will be most useful. Your answer could be:

    a. I'm clear on my mission, and for the next phase I need ...(for example, Trust)

    b. I'm not clear yet on my mission and the state I need next is... (for example, the state of clear thinking; Curiosity; being kind to myself as I explore this; asking myself some important questions; trusting myself; giving myself some time to reflect; trying some new ideas out; accepting that this is a process and will take a little time, etc.)

8. Take yourself back to a time when you deeply experienced these states in the way you've practised throughout the book. Take a few deep breaths as you deeply connect with the states you've chosen. Allow yourself to absorb this feeling into your body, gut, heart, and mind. If there is more than one state required, repeat this step for each one.

9. In a moment, this 'powered up' 'You' and your Inner Coach are going to step together in, and through, that 'Space' that represents your 'Mission'. Feeling those states you chose in step 8, turn towards the 'Space' and step in, and through it. Hear, see, imagine, and feel the presence and support of your Inner Coach walking next to you. Notice how it feels to move in this new way through this area of your life where you used to dû some stuckness.

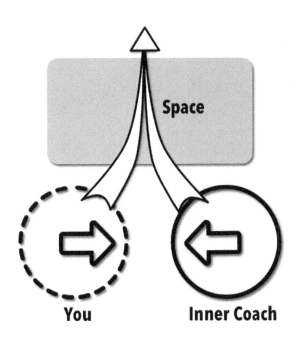

You   **Inner Coach**

10. Step beyond it, to the head of the arrow, with your Inner Coach beside you, and look back, how does it feel to see and experience this change?
11. Staying here, reconnect with the Gateway States of Kindness and Connection again and feel it flowing through you and anyone else involved. Flowing through those old places where you used to dû stuck and healing those moments. Flowing into your future with these new states and an empowered sense of who you are. Notice how you feel different now.

'Let's move on from 'right and wrong'.

CHAPTER 22: ENDING

I do hope you've enjoyed your journey exploring inner wisdom and applying these techniques to make powerful changes in your life. As we reach the final pages of this book, I'd like to reflect on some of the key moments of this journey of connecting with 'The Coach That's Always There'.

We've discovered how much our brain loves change and how change works on a neurological level. Understanding that unlocks so much possibility. Things that we felt were part of our nature or character suddenly become recast as things that we had just become very practised at.

This led us to the fascinating field of States. We discovered that everyone is in a 'State' all the time, but much of the time the state we are in is not the most useful one for achieving what we're trying to achieve. We also identified that for many people, the idea of changing their state at will is an unattainable dream, primarily because no one ever taught them the skills they needed to make this change.

We also started to gain our first insights into how language affects neurology. We identified that setting goals using words that describe exactly what we don't want, makes change difficult and life very hard. For example, saying, 'I don't want to be stressed', makes us think of the things we are dûing stressed about and makes us less relaxed. We also discovered a range of words that we normally assume are positive but turn out to be hidden negatives. These include safe, free, control, etc. and this identifies that we have to be quite focused to spot when we are using words that unintentionally nudge our neurology in the wrong direction.

Next was our exploration of the Gateway States. As we have covered them extensively throughout the book, I'm sure you're now deeply familiar with them and have discovered for yourself how accessing these states changes so much. The first Gateway State we met was 'Trust' and how it is linked to the core idea of IW that you are the Expert on you. This led us to the next Gateway State of Inner Coaching which utilises this 'Trust'. By recognising that we do know more about ourselves than anybody else, and compassionately using the qualities of coaching along with focused questions, we can discover that we have the answers within us. In this section, we began to recognise how physically moving from one space to another, from 'You' to 'Inner Coach', helped us to step out of the troubles that we were entangled with and gain perspective. This powerful approach of using space and movement is such a game changer. I would recommend continuing to use the physical steps and movements of these IWT as much as you can. Although just doing them in your head will work well, physically moving around will have an even bigger benefit.

Next was the Gateway State of 'Self-Kindness'. This incredibly important state is one that many people are unfamiliar with, and in many of the IWTs there was a section on developing Self-Kindness to help increase your connection with this. If when going through IWT, you found that that section had lost a little of its impact through familiarity, then be creative and come up with new ways of being nice to yourself. Change the words until they have meaning for you, as it's so important that each time you genuinely have a sense that your coach is being Kind and is there for you.

The Gateway State of 'Curiosity' followed and opened the conversation about MAPPS. This concept is such an interesting way of framing how we and others can differ. It also highlights how, as all maps are approximate and updateable, maybe we can be more forgiving of others for their current perspectives and can also choose to let go of elements of our map that we no longer want. As MAPPS can be seen everywhere, we considered a range of important ones. These included how we saw our health, what limits we put on change, and how our beliefs, which we often think are stable, are updated throughout our lives. This naturally led to the next Gateway State of 'Shift'. We used 'Shift' to change beliefs within the Compass Process and explored ideas around responsibility and influence, ending with learning the new life-changing verb dû and the powerful 'Given That...' process. The special type of 'Shift' that is the Gateway State of 'Transformation' introduced us to the concept of 'Parts', which is such an important topic that it could have a book that just focused on it. From my experience, I would expect that by applying the Parts IWT you have already noticed some dramatic changes and transformations in things that had been problematic for you for some time. As the Parts IWT can take more than 20-30 minutes to complete, there is a shorter version you can use when time is limited. This involves the first steps of the IWT of noticing the Part and being deeply kind to it. Very often, this will transform how you feel, reduce symptoms, allow emotions to flow and be released, and leave you in a much better place. Later, when you have the time, you may wish to go back and complete the full IWT.

Our final stop on the journey was to look at the Gateway State of 'Connection'. This provided some fascinating approaches for connecting with our IW to deal with others or reconnecting with our sense of purpose and mission. These included the Four Positions, the Wise Ancestor, the Listening Tree, the Magic Carpet, and the journeys through our body, the water and oxygen cycles and the universe...

And that brings us full circle, back to this final chapter.

To finish, I would like to share this story with you and then take you through a final process.

I'd like to take you on a journey to meet a wise old apple tree that grows on the side of a valley formed by a huge, towering mountain. In the spring the bees and other insects visit the tree and help the process of pollination. Its fruit grows and ripens through the summer, and towards the summer's end, the apples gently tumble to the ground. Autumn is followed by the snows of winter, until eventually, spring begins to warm the air again.

One summer, a beautiful, wonderfully plumaged bird with iridescent feathers glides through the forest on the mountainside and lands delicately near the apples. When it's finished enjoying the fruit, it picks up a single seed in its beak and flies off, with its beautiful plumage glistening, soaring higher and higher. Gazing down at the land below, seeing the mountains and the trees, it glides back and rests in its beautiful nest, surveying the landscape. And as it meets its chicks, the tiny seed is forgotten as it falls from its beak. The seed rolls down and lands on a small ledge. The ledge is empty and barren, dry and dusty, and always in shadow. The trees on the other side of the valley are so high that this ledge never sees sunlight.

Seasons come and go, and seed just lies there. One particularly long, hot summer, the orange sun is so strong and the grass so dry and brittle that a fire begins in the forest on the mountainside. The tall trees in this area are the kind that need fire and its intense heat every now and then to allow their seeds to germinate, so, although, on one level, it looks like the forest has been raised and ravaged, a new generation is awakening.

As the ash cloud from the forest fire rises, thick smoke clouds block the sun. The day becomes dark, the birds stop singing, the air chills and an unseasonal rain falls. Eventually, the rain douses the fire, the fire burns out, the smoke disperses, and calm returns. Water and soft ash fall gently, drifting all the way down, some of it coming to rest on the ledge, covering the seed. Now the ledge is no longer as it was. It's been transformed by the dust and rain into thick, warm, luxuriant mud. And so, the seed begins to grow.

Spring comes, and now, in the wake of the fire which has softened the tree line on the valley on the hillside opposite, sunlight reaches the ledge. The apple seed begins to sprout. Year upon year, the young tree grows and becomes taller, and even though the forest on the other side also grows back, it grows just as quickly. It catches the sunlight in its leaves in the summer, it's watered by the winters' melting snow and in spring, one year when it's ready, it blossoms, and fruit grows.

By the end of the summer, mouth-watering apples tumble gently onto the ground beneath it. One day a beautiful bird, with iridescent plumage, softly and easily glides onto the ledge and helps itself to an apple. Taking a seed in its beak, it soars into the sky. The apple tree on the far side of the hill looks at the apple tree on the ledge. It looks at the seed carried away by the bird, and the wise apple tree has seen this all before. It knows, that although sometimes it takes a little while, eventually, all seeds find their place to grow, the right soil to push their roots into, they stretch their stems and leaves, produce fruit, and with the experience of the seasons, become deeply wise.

The final process involves a very simple but powerful question that I would recommend you ask yourself most days and after any significant experience good or less good in your life. For today I recommend using this IWT to focus your attention on this book. Simply take a few moments to get prepared as usual, sitting quietly and taking five deep breaths.

And ask yourself. 'What are the most important things I've learned from this?'

Once you've taken the time to answer fully, then ask:

'And where will this learning be most useful for me?'

Notice your answer and consider how it will make a positive difference to:

1. Your relationships, communications, and the places you go to.
2. Your talents and abilities, actions, and behaviours.
3. The way you spend your time and energy.
4. Other beliefs you have about your future and who you really are.
5. Your ability to show up for others and make an even bigger difference in the things that are deeply important to you.

Thanks for joining me on this journey into Inner Wisdom and getting in touch with The Coach That's Always There. I'd be fascinated to discover how this book has made a difference to you and your future, so please do get in touch to let me know on social media or by email phil@philparker.org .

'We Just Need To Remember That 'The Coach That's Always There'.'

APPENDIX AND REFERENCES

COACHING QUALITIES

This list is abridged from my book, the 10 Questions to Ask for Success.

Coach - This is a specific type of role that one person adopts to assist someone else to sort out their issues.

The qualities that ensure the assistance is coaching rather than advice or interference are:

1. Coaching is only provided when there has been a clear request or an agreement for coaching.
2. The coach leaves their own problems at the door.
3. The coach clearly believes in their coachee.
4. The coach will assess the feasibility of the coachee's plans. If they believe them to be sound and achievable, they will let their coachee know that.
5. The coach always maintains a big, clear perspective, which will often be bigger and clearer than the coachee's. This allows them to see the endpoint even when their coachee can't.
6. The coach doesn't take any bulls***. If their coachee has committed to achieving something and begins to cheat on themselves, talk themselves down, or not deliver on their promises they won't stand for it.
7. The coach rarely gives advice, but mainly asks questions that assist their coachee to discover the solutions.
8. The coach is supportive and caring.
9. The coach listens but will assist their coachee to refocus if they start to go off the point or endlessly complain.
10. The coach takes the time because they know their coachee is important.
11. The coach has integrity, they don't just say things, they really mean them.
12. The coach lets their coachee know they understand what is going on for them and that the success of the coachee is important to them.
13. The coach will give feedback instead of criticism and never say 'you're wrong' (this is an identity level statement, which implies

the coachee is wrong, rather than what they did was inappropriate), although they may suggest improvements to aspects of their performance.
14. The coach is able to reflect on both their and their coachee performance.
15. The coach brings a sense of humour and lightness to the situation.

REFERENCES

For ease of access to all the references in the book please visit philparker.org/IW

ABOUT THE AUTHOR

Dr. Phil Parker

PhD, DO, Dip E Hyp P NLP, Certified Master Trainer of NLP

Dr. Phil Parker is a lecturer, therapist and innovator in the field of the mind-body connection. He designed Lightning Process® seminars, which are now available in 16 different countries. He is an Osteopath, brief solution therapist, coach, Ericksonian Hypnotherapist and Master Trainer in NLP, and gained his PhD in the Psychology of Health researching a new NLP/LP based approach for addictions. He is the principal of the Phil Parker Training Institute and held a lecturing and research post at London Metropolitan University.

He has worked with performers at the highest level, including Premiership footballers, European Tour golfers, the British Olympic medical team and was the performance psychologist for Ed Stafford's successful Guinness World Record attempt to walk the Amazon. He has authored a number of papers and four books on NLP, LP, coaching and health, which have been translated into a range of languages.

He is passionate about helping others make change and his superpower is communicating complex ideas in an intriguing and easy-to-understand way.

Made in the USA
Middletown, DE
15 September 2023

38568741R00146